THE
PSALM
112
PROMISE

THE
PSALM
112
PROMISE

JOHN ECKHARDT

CHARISMA
HOUSE

Most CHARISMA HOUSE BOOK GROUP products are available at special quantity discounts for bulk purchase for sales promotions, premiums, fund-raising, and educational needs. For details, write Charisma House Book Group, 600 Rinehart Road, Lake Mary, Florida 32746, or telephone (407) 333-0600.

THE PSALM 112 PROMISE by John Eckhardt
Published by Charisma House
Charisma Media/Charisma House Book Group
600 Rinehart Road
Lake Mary, Florida 32746
www.charismahouse.com

Cover design by Justin Evans

Visit the author's website at www.johneckhardt.global.

Library of Congress Cataloging-in-Publication Data:
An application to register this book for cataloging has been
submitted to the Library of Congress.
International Standard Book Number: 978-1-62999-474-1
E-book ISBN: 978-1-62999-475-8

18 19 20 21 22 — 9 8 7 6 5 4 3 2 1
Printed in the United States of America

CONTENTS

Introduction

GOD'S PROMISE TO THE STABLE BELIEVER

Blessed is the man who fears the LORD, who delights greatly in His commandments. His offspring shall be mighty in the land; the generation of the upright shall be blessed. Wealth and riches shall be in his house, and his righteousness endures forever. To the upright there arises light in the darkness; he is gracious, and full of compassion, and righteous. A good man shows generous favor, and lends; he will guide his affairs with justice. Surely the righteous man shall not be moved; the righteous shall be in everlasting remembrance. He shall not be afraid of evil tidings; his heart is fixed, trusting in the LORD. His heart is established; he shall not be afraid, until he sees triumph upon his enemies. He has given away freely; he has given to the poor; his righteousness endures forever; his horn shall be exalted with honor. The wicked shall see it and be grieved; he shall gnash his teeth and melt away; the desire of the wicked shall perish.
—PSALM 112:1–10

P SALM 112 HAS been one of my favorite psalms for a long time. These ten verses reveal the blessings and the characteristics of a person who fears the Lord and delights greatly in His commandments. I call this person a spiritually stable believer—one who is fixed and established in the Lord, single-minded, steadfast, and righteous.

One of the hallmarks of my ministry is teaching people how to be set free from the traps and bondages of the enemy. Since the creation of man, the enemy's goal has been to keep us from everything God has promised and purposed for our lives. At the root of his attacks is an effort to shake us and make us insecure and unstable in our trust and faith in God. This is what the Bible calls double-mindedness: "A double-minded man is unstable in all his ways" (James 1:8). Rejection opens the door to double-mindedness. Rejection shakes us from knowing who we are in Christ. Then comes rebellion, which keeps us from willingly and lovingly following and obeying God. This is the core of a double-minded person: rejection and rebellion.

But the heart of a person who fears the Lord is fixed, established, sure, and confident. Mirroring God's character in love and holiness, his heart does not reject or rebel against the things of God. He welcomes the full measure of salvation and therefore reaps many benefits. This is the person Psalm 112 reveals to us. He is gracious, full of compassion, and generous. He cannot be moved. He is uncompromisingly and consistently righteous. His righteousness endures forever.

This psalm provides the standard to which all stable believers should aspire. Becoming like the man of Psalm 112 should be our goal. This man is a type of Christ, and the characteristics or traits that this passage reveals cannot be achieved except in Christ. These verses reveal the key to being truly prosperous from the inside out—prosperous in the sense that God intends for all His people.

Many of the lessons and principles taught on prosperity do not teach it from the perspective of someone who is prosperous from within. The Bible says that we are to prosper even as our souls prosper. Prosperity is more than financial abundance or having a lot of money. You can have money and no prosperity. If your marriage and other relationships are messed up—if your mind, body, and/or spirit is messed up and you have no peace—then you are not prospering.

PROSPERITY FLOWS FROM THE INSIDE OUT

Prosperity is a result of salvation. Prosperity is part of our covenant with God and is the full manifestation of *shalom*, or peace, which in the Hebrew means wholeness, health and healing, favor, and a blessed life. Shalom means you enjoy relationships—*healthy* relationships. You enjoy a healthy mind and body, and healthy finances. True prosperity is a result of prospering on the inside.

Anytime you are not prospering, don't look to blame anyone or anything else; look on the inside. Ask God to show you what is not stable in your life and in your heart.

> Examine me, O LORD, and test me; try my affections and my heart.
>
> —PSALM 26:2

> Search me, O God, and know my heart; try me, and know my concerns, and see if there is any rebellious way in me, and lead me in the ancient way.
>
> —PSALM 139:23–24

Ask God to show you if there is anything you need to be healed of and delivered from so that what's on the inside can manifest on the outside.

> Beloved, I pray that all may go well with you and that you may be in good health, even as your soul is well.
>
> —3 John 2

If you are not prosperous on the inside, then any outward prosperity you obtain will be destroyed. You cannot sustain outward prosperity without being inwardly stable. There are a lot of people who are trying to prosper financially, physically, and mentally. They work on their bodies by eating healthy and exercising. They work toward having peace and a sound mind. They want to prosper. They believe it is God's will for them to prosper. Yet it is amazing to me how many of these same people who prophesy, speak in tongues, cast out demons, are saved, love the Lord, are in the Word and filled with the Holy Ghost, praise God, worship, and do everything they are taught to do are not prospering in their health, in their minds, in their finances, or in their relationships. They're unhappy, unsatisfied, confused, and mixed up. They are not prospering.

AN ISSUE OF THE HEART

The truth is that our lives are the direct result of what is in our hearts. The more I've studied double-mindedness, the more I realize it is not only about indecision, doubting, wavering, and inconsistency, but it is also something that is characteristic of the wicked, people who are far from God for whatever reason. Though we may try to normalize it, insecurity and double-mindedness are not normal or good. They are greatly limiting to a full and enjoyable life.

In the two places the letter of James talks about double-mindedness, the writer applies this word to someone who has something impure in his heart:

> A double-minded man is unstable in all his ways.
>
> —James 1:8

> Cleanse your hands, you sinners, and purify your hearts, you double-minded.
>
> —James 4:8

Throughout the Scriptures double-minded people are equated with sinful, wicked people. In Psalm 119:113, the psalmist says, "I hate those who are double-minded, but I love Your law," drawing a parallel between stable-mindedness and obedience to God.

Double-mindedness is not the characteristic of a godly person. God only wants the abundant life for us, which is why He made deliverance from double-mindedness possible. He wants our hearts to be whole so that our lives can be whole.

When we see a person's life messed up, it is usually because his heart is messed up. The Bible says, "Keep your heart with all diligence, for out of it are the issues of life" (Prov. 4:23). The heart, in spiritual terms, is more than a physical pump for circulating blood through the body. The heart the Bible refers to is a person's mind and spirit—the center of one's being. Out of this center flow the issues of life.

We cannot keep operating under the false assumption that we all have good hearts when the fruit of our lives is not good. Yes, we may have good motives from time to time, but if we are living messed-up lives, then our hearts are not good. We need a change of heart.

Your heart controls what comes out in your life. It's important to make sure that your heart, soul, and mind are right. That's what deliverance is for: to restore your soul and to deal with something on the inside of you that causes your heart not to be right, whether it be rejection, rebellion, fear, anger, lust, hatred, resentment, bitterness, unforgiveness, envy, paranoia, selfishness, distrust, or whatever issue it is. If those things are in your heart, they are going to affect that way you live, from relationships to lifestyle to prosperity. You will not prosper the way God wants you to if you do not prosper on the inside first.

THE PROMISE OF A
STABLE AND PROSPEROUS LIFE

Mark the blameless ["perfect," KJV] man, and consider the upright, for the end of that man is peace.
—PSALM 37:37

"Perfect" is what the Bible identifies as complete, mature, godly, and consistent.[1] Perfect or upright men and women love God and love others. They have made a decision to follow the wisdom of God, and it guides everything they do. If anything comes up in their lives that challenges God's wisdom, they have already made up their mind to reject it. This is what stable-minded, upright believers do. This is how they live their lives.

Many people want the blessings of Psalm 112 but don't want to do what it takes to get their hearts purified so that they prosper from the inside out. Obedience and commitment to God is what it takes, and in this book we are going to study the level of commitment required to be considered a Psalm 112 believer and the blessings that come with this lifestyle.

Each chapter in this book will focus on one concept presented in the verses of Psalm 112. Each verse or set of verses contains attributes of the stable believer as well as the promises of God associated with the one who exemplifies these attributes. Many of the promises of God come in the form of an if-then relationship. For example, Isaiah 1:19 says, "If you are willing and obedient, [then] you shall eat the best of the land" (AMP). As we do our part—be "willing and obedient"—*then* God will bless us by allowing us to "eat the best of the land."

God is always faithful to keep His promises. He never wavers. Deuteronomy 7:9 says, "Know therefore that the LORD your God, He is God, the faithful God, who keeps covenant and mercy with them who love Him and keep His commandments to a thousand generations." *Covenant* in this verse is synonymous with God's promise, pledge, or agreement with His children to reward us as we remain faithful to Him and His ways.

As we examine Psalm 112, we will see that it is set up with the same structure as a covenantal agreement. We live as God commands—holy, righteous, and upright; we become stable, fixed, established, and immovable in Him—and He releases His promises. Here is a snapshot of the Psalm 112 promise:

1. If we fear God, then our lives will be blessed (v. 1).

2. If we worship God through obedience (v. 1, AMP), then we will have generational blessing and increase (v. 2).

3. If we intimately know the God we serve, then we will have more than enough. Wealth and riches will dwell in our houses (v. 3).

4. If we operate with grace and compassion, then light will shine on the dark places in our lives (v. 4).

5. If we guide our affairs with wisdom ("discretion," KJV) and justice (fairness, honesty, wisdom), then good will come to us (v. 5, NLT). We will live prosperous and successful lives.

6. If we remain uncompromisingly righteous, then we will not be overcome by

   evil (NLT) and we will be remembered
   forever (v. 6).

7. If we remain fixed, trusting in God, then
   our hearts will be established and we
   will triumph over the enemy (vv. 7–8).

8. If we give generously (NLT), then we will
   be exalted with honor (v. 9).

The first three aspects of the Psalm 112 promise are about God—our fear and honor of God, our relationship with Him, and our knowing His character and His ways intimately. The last five are about our character, our faithfulness to God, and our commitment to consistently live out the changes and transformations His Spirit brings to our lives.

Becoming like the man in Psalm 112 is our goal. This man is a type of Christ, and the characteristics or traits this passage reveals cannot be achieved except in Christ by the power and grace of the Holy Spirit. These verses reveal the keys to being truly prosperous—living a life of wholeness, peace, favor, and health in your relationships, your mind, your body, and your finances. Let's go deeper into each one to see how we can live in the Psalm 112 promise.

Chapter 1

THE CONSEQUENCES OF AN UNSTABLE LIFE

He who wavers is like a wave of the sea, driven and tossed with the wind. Let not that man think that he will receive anything from the Lord. A double-minded man is unstable in all his ways.
—JAMES 1:6–8

Given a choice—bad news or good news first—most people say, "Give me the good news first." For them, it makes the bad news easier to handle. I'm not going to do that here. I am going to give you the bad news first so you can enjoy the rest of this journey, which is all good news. I'm starting with the bad or hard news first because I want you to see why it is important to come into agreement with God to live a stable and holy life. When you see that the way you've been living on your own causes more hardship with few rewards and blessings, you will appreciate it more when you discover the other way—the way of the stable, single-minded Psalm 112 believer.

You do not have to live an unstable, double-minded life. You do not have to live in a state of constant internal and external havoc, doubting and wavering about if God cares or if He will come through for you.

Sometimes we respond to others and to ourselves as if this kind of insecurity is normal, that this is just how life will be. "Well, you can't ever be too sure," many of us have said. Sometimes we excuse the manifestations of double-mindedness and spiritual instability as normal. We think being inconsistent is natural and everyone is just like that. We accept it. But to be one way one minute and the total opposite another is not godly. People cannot trust that. When you are like that—a roller coaster of emotions, in and out of relationships, always in conflict or confusion—then you will not be able to prosper in life. Your life will be absent of abiding joy and peace. This is not God's way for you to live.

We cannot compromise and settle for inconsistency in living according to the Word of God. Like the Psalm 112 man, our righteousness should continue forever. This is our modus operandi as believers—consistency and stability.

So, yes, we'll start with the bad news. We will get it out of the way quickly, because this is not where we want to dwell. But many of us need to see what we're doing wrong to clearly see what to do that is right and what will bring blessing and success to our lives and the lives of those we love and influence. This picture may be one you are well familiar with and tired of. It's a picture of the life that you don't have to live any longer, the life that does not match God's plan for you, and the life Jesus did not die on the cross to give you. We will look at an unstable life from three perspectives:

1. Your relationship with yourself

2. Your relationship with others

3. Your relationship with God

THE UNSTABLE YOU

Have you ever caught yourself acting at times in polar opposites? Maybe you are the minister who is godly, prayerful, and holy at times yet has periods of sin, doubt, and struggles with lust. Maybe you are the believer who lives a strong Christian life but has seasons of backsliding. Or maybe you are the person who is outgoing and cheerful yet falls into bouts of withdrawal and depression. The person who is hard working and a perfectionist yet has periods of lethargy and sloppiness. The person who is gentle and kind but has periods of outburst and rage. It is almost as if you are two

THE PSALM 112 PROMISE

people. This is double-mindedness, the kind of instability that manifests when you have not established yourself in God.

The Greek phrase for *double-minded* (*dipsuchos*) literally means "double souled," from *dis*, meaning "twice," and *psuche*, meaning "mind."[1] Having two minds is the description of confusion. Confusion is a lack of understanding; uncertainty, a situation of panic; a breakdown of order.

Here I am going to highlight the most common way that we display double-mindedness throughout our lives.

A love of the world

According to James 4, double-mindedness is like an internal war with ourselves. We can look like lovers of God on the outside but be enemies of God in our hearts. James says that this is because even after we were saved, we maintained friendship with the world (v. 4). We try to be religious and love God, and simultaneously chase after passions in the world. Out of this dichotomy come things we see in our lives and relationships, from our home lives to public interactions, small scale to large scale and everything in between.

> You adulterers and adulteresses, do you not
> know that the friendship with the world is
> enmity with God? Whoever therefore will be
> a friend of the world is the enemy of God.
> —JAMES 4:4

In the introduction I talked about the two-sided spirits that make up double-mindedness: rejection and rebellion. It is the rejection side of the double-minded personality that weds a person to the world for love. It is simply Satan's substitute for true love. Double-mindedness breeds worldliness and carnality.

Rebellion as a teenager

Worldliness can be seen in teenage rebellion. If you recall your teenage years, you may remember your desire to get involved in a lifestyle of lust, perversion, drugs, or other behaviors that were opposite the way you were raised. If you are a parent of a teenager, you may see this rebellion in them. Teenage rebellion often leaves parents at their wits' end. Signs of double-mindedness can be seen in piercings, tattoos, punk dressing, goth dressing, provocative clothing, drug addiction, smoking, running away, fighting, gang activity, profanity, disrespect to authority, alternative lifestyles, depression, suicidal tendencies, and withdrawal.

For a generation now, disruptive young Americans who rebel against authority figures have been increasingly diagnosed with mental illnesses and medicated with psychiatric (psychotropic) drugs. Disruptive young people who are medicated with Ritalin, Adderall and other amphetamines routinely report that these drugs make them "care less" about their boredom, resentments and other negative emotions, thus making them more compliant and manageable. And so-called atypical anti-psychotics such as Risperdal and Zyprexa—powerful tranquilizing drugs—are increasingly prescribed to disruptive young Americans, even though in most cases they are not displaying any psychotic symptoms.[2]

Teenage double-mindedness has become an epidemic. Most don't know what they are dealing with. God's solution is deliverance and healing. Double-mindedness has also been called passive-aggression, but it is simply rejection/rebellion.

Indecision

If it is displeasing to you to serve the LORD, then *choose* today whom you will serve, if it should be the gods your fathers served

> beyond the River or the gods of the Amorites'
> land where you are now living. Yet as for me
> and my house, we will serve the LORD.
> —JOSHUA 24:15, EMPHASIS ADDED

Double-mindedness causes indecision, which results in procrastination, compromise, confusion, forgetfulness, and indifference. Indecision is one of the most debilitating problems in life because life is based on decisions. Indifference is an attitude that causes a person to avoid making decisions. Procrastination is another way of avoiding decisions by just putting them off for a future time. It can also be rooted in the fear of making a decision. In addition to this is the fear of making the *wrong* choice.

Our choices pave the way for success or failure. A double-minded person has a difficult time making decisions and often changes his or her mind after making a decision. This results in wavering and always questioning one's own decisions.

> I call heaven and earth to witnesses against
> you this day, that I have set before you life
> and death, blessing and curse. Therefore
> choose life, that both you and your descen-
> dants may live.
> —DEUTERONOMY 30:19

The Word of God challenges us to make wise decisions. We are commanded to choose life. We can choose blessing or cursing. We can choose the fear of the Lord. We can choose to serve the Lord.

Our life is the result of our choices. We choose our paths in life. We choose whom we marry. When we have children, we influence what they will choose as they get older. We choose the jobs we will work, the friends we will have, and the places we will live. The Bible is filled with examples of men and women who made bad choices and suffered the consequences. It also shows us the blessing of wise choices.

The double-minded person is often paralyzed when it comes to making choices. Have you ever been around those who can't decide what they want to do in life? It is frustrating to say the least. This can be a sign of double-mindedness and the need for deliverance. Proper decision-making is the result of wisdom and a stable personality.

Poor health

> A merry heart does good like a medicine, but
> a broken spirit dries the bones.
> —PROVERBS 17:22

Chris Simpson of New Wine Media teaches on the effects the double-minded stronghold of rejection can have on your physical health. He says:

> Did you know that rejection can affect you physically? It can dry up your bones. Generally, it's the "internalizers" that tend to get sick from their rejection. Why is that? It's because rejection often produces anger. And you have to do something with your anger. If you bury it inside, it'll find a way to the surface. If you live in denial concerning your anger, then you'll be resentful and bitter. These attitudes can bring physical problems.
>
> I've often seen people healed on the spot when they forgave those that had hurt them, and when they renounced the bitterness and resentment in their heart. It's amazing how quickly the Holy Spirit will heal and bring life to the dried bones. Many sicknesses and physical maladies tend to be rooted in rejection and bitterness: skin problems, headaches, allergies, neck or back aches, stiffness of joints, arthritis, pains, stress, nervousness, and various diseases.[3]

What he shares here I have seen as well in my almost forty years of deliverance ministry. When I have laid hands on an individual to bring deliverance from bitterness, anger, and unforgiveness, I have found that rejection and rebellion are at the root of their issues. They often get healed from various physical ailments such as heart disease, some cancers, arthritis, and more when they forgive and release bitterness.

It is the rejection part of double-mindedness that can lead to self-rejection, which will manifest as illness in the body. We are seeing a rise in the diagnosis of autoimmune diseases, and the cause for much of it is said to be unknown. Autoimmune diseases occur when the immune system begins to attack the body. Thyroiditis, arthritis, type 1 diabetes, certain cancers and heart diseases, lupus, various allergies, and asthma are kinds of autoimmune diseases. Autoimmune symptoms often manifest after a person experiences a devastating loss, endures trauma, or is excessively stressed over a period of time.

If you have been dealing with recurring illness and have not been able to find a cure, seek out a deliverance minister or begin to ask the Lord to help you uncover some hurt in your life that may lie at the root of your illness.

THE UNSTABLE YOU AND OTHERS

Instability with your place in God can result in a lifetime of bad relationships. Relationships and covenants require stability. Unstable people will have a difficult time developing long-lasting, stable relationships. This affects marriages as well and is the real cause of many divorces. This instability affects families and children, who need stable parents and a stable home environment in which to grow.

Unstable people make unstable marriage partners

Double-mindedness affects our ability to honor and stay true to covenant. Covenant requires stability, loyalty, and faithfulness. How can we walk in covenant if we are double-minded? How can we have strong covenant relationships if we are double-minded?

Marriage is a covenant between a husband and a wife. Is it any wonder that we have so many divorces in and out of the church? There are too many unstable people entering into marriages. Double-minded people will have instability in their marriages. We will continue to see troubled marriages unless double-mindedness is dealt with. With such a large number of marriages ending in divorce, it is no surprise that double-mindedness is a major problem.

Unstable men make unstable husbands and fathers

There are a lot of double-minded men who are married and have children. Families need strong, steadfast men. Men are called to be the providers and protectors of the family. When trouble comes, the husband and father should be able to stand up and say, "Honey, I got this. Don't worry, baby. Children, don't worry. It's all right. I believe God. I pray. I bind. I loose. I take authority over the devil. I'm the head of my house. Devil, you cannot have my wife, my kids, or my family. You will not destroy us, because I trust in God. I am the covering. I am the head of this house."

Yet too frequently we find weak, double-minded men who let their wives go to church and do all the praying and believing, while they stay home watching football. Then when spiritual trouble comes, they don't know how to pray, bind the devil, loose, stand up for anything, or recite a scripture. They leave their families vulnerable to attack.

They are drunkards, whoremongers, liars, and cheaters. They don't want to get married, raise their children, or keep covenant. This is how double-mindedness affects the most critical relationships in our society.

THE UNSTABLE YOU AND GOD

God is a covenant-keeping God, and our relationship with Him is based on covenant. Double-mindedness makes it impossible to have a stable, loyal, and intimate relationship with God. We become wavering, unbelieving, and backsliding people who are unable to be firmly planted in Him.

There have been times in my ministry when I kept seeing the same person come again and again to the altar to get saved. I would wonder, "How many times are you going to come back to the Lord? How many times are you going to come to the altar? How many times are you going to be the prodigal son? How many times are you going to be in the pigpen? Where is your consistency with God?"

We can't be happy with a life like this. It is hard to be out of step with God once you had been in step with Him. When we backslide, we deal with torment. We can't rest or be at peace because our hearts have known the fellowship of God. Who wants to live a life they can't enjoy?

This on-again, off-again commitment to God is a pattern in many believers' lives. I have seen believers commit to Christ and then turn away and return to the world. They then return and repeat the process over again. It is heartbreaking.

Unbelief and backsliding are signs of double-mindedness, wavering between two lifestyles. They were also the issues of those in the early church who were departing from the faith. Many of the Hebrews were returning to the Old Covenant system. They were wavering in their faith. Wavering is a sign of double-mindedness.

CHECK YOURSELF

Are you double-minded in your walk with Christ? Do you have a history of backsliding and departing from the faith? Are you guilty of worldliness and carnality? Do you crack under pressure or persecution and return to the things of the world? These are all signs of double-mindedness that can make it hard to deal with the challenges that often come with being a believer. How many times have you felt like a storm was raging inside of you? James 1:6 describes double-mindedness as being like a storm:

> But let him ask in faith, without wavering.
> For he who wavers is like a wave of the sea,
> driven and tossed with the wind.

Do you have a history of stormy relationships? If you are a minister or leader, are there always storms in your church or within your team or organization? If the answer is yes, then the problem is double-mindedness.

The Holy Spirit is beginning to show you some double-minded tendencies in your life. The Lord is calling you to have more stability in certain areas. Do not dismiss the conviction of the Lord. He chastens those He loves. It is God's love and grace that call us to repentance. Through repentance and deliverance we are able to establish secure footing in Him. We are able to walk upright and receive the full benefits of being His child.

That was the hard news. Now I encourage you to continue through the next parts of this book with prayer and expectation as the Lord shows you His promises for you as you commit to being rooted and grounded in Him and His ways.

PRAYERS TO BREAK
THE SPIRIT OF DOUBLE-MINDEDNESS

I bind and rebuke every spirit that would attempt to distort, disturb, or disintegrate the development of my personality in the name of Jesus.

I break all curses of schizophrenia and double-mindedness on my family in the name of Jesus.

I bind and rebuke the spirit of double-mindedness in the name of Jesus (James 1:8).

I bind and take authority over the strongmen of rejection and rebellion, and separate them in the name of Jesus.

I bind and cast out the spirits of rejection, fear of rejection, and self-rejection in the name of Jesus.

I bind and cast out all spirits of lust, fantasy, harlotry, and perverseness in the name of Jesus.

I bind and cast out all spirits of insecurity and inferiority in the name of Jesus.

I bind and cast out all spirits of self-accusation and compulsive confession in the name of Jesus.

I bind and cast out all spirits of fear of judgment, self-pity, false compassion, and false responsibility in the name of Jesus.

I bind and cast out all spirits of depression, despondency, despair, discouragement, and hopelessness in the name of Jesus.

I bind and cast out all spirits of guilt, condemnation, unworthiness, and shame in the name of Jesus.

I bind and cast out all spirits of perfection, pride, vanity, ego, intolerance, frustration, and impatience in the name of Jesus.

I bind and cast out all spirits of unfairness, withdrawal, pouting, unreality, fantasy, daydreaming, and vivid imagination in the name of Jesus.

I bind and cast out all spirits of self-awareness, timidity, loneliness, and sensitivity in the name of Jesus.

I bind and cast out all spirits of talkativeness, nervousness, tension, and fear in the name of Jesus.

I bind and cast out all spirits of self-will, selfishness, and stubbornness in the name of Jesus.

I bind and cast out the spirit of accusation in the name of Jesus.

I bind and cast out all spirits of self-delusion, self-deception, and self-seduction in the name of Jesus.

I bind and cast out all spirits of judgment, pride, and unteachableness in the name of Jesus.

I bind and cast out all spirits of control and possessiveness in the name of Jesus.

I bind and cast out the root of bitterness in the name of Jesus.

I bind and cast out all spirits of hatred, resentment, violence, murder, unforgiveness, anger, and retaliation in the name of Jesus.

I bind and cast out spirits of paranoia, suspicion, distrust, persecution, confrontation, and fear in the name of Jesus.

Chapter 2

BLESSED

Blessed [fortunate, prosperous, and favored by God] is the man who fears the LORD [with awe-inspired reverence and worships Him with obedience], who delights greatly in His commandments.
—PSALM 112:1, AMP

WHEN ASKED WHAT they want out of life, many people say, "I just want to be happy." Maybe you've said the same thing. In the Bible, the word *blessed* is synonymous with *happiness*.[1] If you think about it, whether we are believers or unbelievers, we spend most of our lives in pursuit of happiness. It is even the basis of the United States Declaration of Independence: "We hold these truths to be self-evident, that all men are created equal, that they are endowed by their Creator with certain unalienable Rights, that among these are Life, Liberty and the pursuit of Happiness."[2] Although being blessed and happy is a pursuit endowed by God, we don't experience it enough.

Happiness has become so hard to find that we have come to believe and expect that it is unattainable. Because we are miserable, we make others feel guilty when they are happy or satisfied. But the person who is stable and established in God is happy. They are the ones who have found God's wisdom and understanding (Prov. 3:13). They are the ones who love God's correction and do not despise His instruction (Job 5:17). They despise sin but have mercy on the poor (Prov. 14:21). They handle matters wisely and trust in the Lord (Prov. 16:20). They are fruitful and multiply (Ps. 127:5). They eat the fruit of their labor, and all goes well with them (Ps. 128:2). Their God is the Lord (Ps. 144:15, KJV). They have the God of Jacob for their help. Their hope is in the Lord (Ps. 146:5, KJV). They keep the law of God and the law of the land (Prov. 29:18, KJV). They are the ones whom the Lord has saved. He is their shield and their sword (Deut. 33:29, KJV).

What we see here, then, is that being happy and living a blessed life come down to our position in God. When we are in line with God, we are at peace with Him. We have come into agreement with Him concerning the way He has designed us to live. This is what it means to be in covenant with God. The Psalm 112 man does not waver in his commitment to God. He remains in agreement with God's plan for his life, therefore he is blessed, happy, satisfied, and content.

GOD WANTS YOU TO BE HAPPY

God's thoughts concerning your peace and happiness are much higher than you could imagine. It is His desire to bless and prosper you, to give you His grace, favor, and protection. Unfortunately, some people believe God doesn't want us to be happy. Have you heard people say, "God doesn't want you to be happy; He wants you to be holy"? They make it seem like holiness is punishment, that it is unpleasant to follow God. The Psalm 112 promise challenges that kind of thinking.

Holiness—being set right—is happiness in God's mind. We may have the wrong idea of what it means to be happy. We can easily say, "I am blessed and highly favored." Religious people say this all the time without really thinking about what it means. But how easy is it to honestly say, "I am happy"? We have become so bound in our thinking about God wanting to bless us. It is the way of the transgressor that is hard (Prov. 13:15). The double-minded, bitter, rebellious, confused, and angry person has a hard life, but happy is the man or woman who puts his or her trust in the Lord.

We need to understand that God moved heaven and earth to bring peace and happiness into our lives. This is not to say that pain and disappointment won't come, but God's desire is to give you shalom—the full measure of peace. This is His gift to you as His child. God blesses His people and rescues them. It's just what He does. It takes faith to believe that God wants us to be blessed and live good lives. It takes faith to shut out the lies of the enemy that tell us that following God is miserable, dry, and hard.

Happy people are prosperous

Blessed people are prosperous, and while we will learn in a later chapter that wealth and riches dwell in their houses, prosperity is more than money. In addition to having more than enough provision, it also means having prosperous relationships, having a sound mind, and being able to rest at night—no guilt, no condemnation, no shame, and no fear. Prosperity means that you have all that you need and there is nothing broken in your life. Some people have money, but their minds, hearts, relationships, and marriages are broken. Financial blessing is only part of the picture. There is a holistic life of prosperity that we should be living.

RENEW YOUR MIND CONCERNING BLESSING AND PROSPERITY

Many in the body of Christ shy away from the concept of prosperity, but the Bible doesn't. One of the things I hope to break with the message of this book is the idea that God wants you to just get by, to just have enough to make it, and that anything more is unholy. The Bible says the wealth of the wicked is stored up for the righteous (Prov. 13:22). It says that Christ became poor so that we would be rich (2 Cor. 8:9)—rich in spirit and rich in the natural. God takes pleasure in the prosperity of His servants (Ps. 35:27).

One way to fight back against wrong mind-sets about God's desire for His people is to study the Word. God's Word illuminates His will and opens our ears to hear what His Spirit is trying to say to us. Our minds need to be renewed according to the Spirit, and this happens by reading and meditating on His Word. This needs to happen more and more regarding prosperity and the blessing of God.

I have done extensive research on blessing and prosperity, and I have found that scriptures for these concepts are found in almost every book of the Bible. I believe this reveals how much God desires them for us.

Let's look at some biblical definitions of key words that relate to prosperity, blessing, and peace.

Prosperity, blessing, and peace in the Old Testament

The Old Testament was mostly written in Hebrew.

1. *Běrakah* (Deut. 28:2) is the Hebrew word for *blessing*. It means a blessing, liberal, pool, present. It is from the word *barak*, meaning benediction; by implication prosperity—blessing, liberal, pool, present, peace, generous.[3]

2. *Sakal* (Deut. 29:9) is the Aramaic word often translated "prosper." It means to be prudent, circumspect, have insight, act wisely, give attention to, cause to prosper.[4]

3. *Tsalach* (Ps. 118:25) is a Hebrew word meaning to advance, prosper, make progress, be successful.[5]

4. *Chayil* (Deut. 8:17–18) is a Hebrew word meaning strength, might, efficiency, wealth, force, and army.[6]

5. *Shalah* (Ps. 122:6) is a Hebrew word meaning to be at rest, be quiet, prosper.[7]

6. *Shalowm* (Isa. 9:7) is the Hebrew word meaning peace, harmony, wholeness, completeness, prosperity, and welfare.[8]

7. *Ravah* (Ps. 36:8) is the Hebrew word meaning satisfied, to be full, to have plenty, abundantly satisfied.[9]

8. *Koach* (Deut. 8:18) is the Hebrew word for *power* meaning strength, produce, wealth.[10]

9. *Kabad* (Isa. 60:13) is the Hebrew word for *glory* meaning honor, riches, wealth, weight, splendor.[11]

10. *Hown* (Ps. 112:3) is the Hebrew word for *wealth* meaning an abundance of valuable possessions or money or enough substance.[12]

11. *Ratsown* (Ps. 5:12) is the Hebrew word for *favor* meaning goodwill; "a gracious, friendly, or obliging act that is freely granted."[13]

12. *Gamal* (Ps. 13:6) is the Hebrew word for *bountiful* meaning "liberal in bestowing

gifts, favors, or bounties; munificent; generous."[14]

13. *Esher* (Deut. 33:29) is the Hebrew word for *happy* meaning to become happy, happiness, blessedness.[15] Leah named her son Asher (Gen. 30:13), a variant of *ashar*.[16]

14. *Tuwshiyah* (Prov. 8:14) is the Hebrew word for *wisdom* meaning sound or efficient wisdom and abiding success.[17]

15. *Shalal* (2 Chron. 20:25) is the Hebrew word for *booty* or *spoils* meaning great gain or plunder, the spoils or reward of war.[18]

Prosperity, blessing, and peace in the New Testament

The New Testament was mostly written in Greek.

1. *Eulogeō* (Acts 3:26) is the Greek word meaning bless, to make happy, and to bestow blessings.[19]

2. *Therizō* (John 4:36) is the Greek word meaning to reap, as in reaping a harvest.[20]

3. *Euodoō* (3 John 2) is the Greek word meaning "to help on one's way," to prosper, "to have a prosperous journey," literally or figuratively.[21]

4. *Apekdyomai* (Col. 2:15) is the Greek word meaning arms stripped from an enemy; to disarm and to spoil or plunder one's enemy.[22]

5. *Empiplēmi* (Acts 14:17) is the Greek word meaning to fill up, to fill full, to fill abundantly, to satisfy.[23]

6. *Diathēkē* (Heb. 8:6) is the Greek word meaning covenant—"the last disposition which one makes of his earthly possessions after his death, a testament or will."[24]

7. *Plēthynō* (Acts 6:7) is the Greek word meaning to increase, to multiply.[25]

8. *Perisseuma* (2 Cor. 8:14) is the Greek word meaning abundance, the residue of abundance, the remains, to delight in the residue of abundance.[26]

9. *Autarkeia* (2 Cor. 9:8) is the Greek word meaning divine sufficiency, fully supplied of all our needs.[27]

10. *Dynamis* (2 Cor. 9:10–12) is the Greek word meaning supernatural power, the divine ability to multiply, heal, and working of miracles.[28]

You will see these words, ideas, and scriptures repeated throughout the book. These definitions will help expand your understanding of the whole realm of prosperity—the spiritual blessings as well as natural blessings.

Another key verse for prosperity is Proverbs 10:22: "The blessing of the LORD makes rich, and He adds no sorrow with it." This goes back to God wanting us to enjoy life, to enjoy His blessing, and to be happy and at peace.

The opposite of prosperity is lack, want, poverty, emptiness, barrenness, bankruptcy, backsliding, oppression, bondage, captivity, slavery, sadness, defeat, stagnation, failure, and shame. A lot of these look like the double-minded manifestations I mentioned in the first chapter of this book. The stable-minded enjoy the blessings of peace and prosperity.

I encourage you to look up each scripture from the two previous lists and form your own set of confessions to help you receive revelation of God's desire for you to be blessed and happy.

BLESSED, HAPPY, AND PROSPEROUS PEOPLE ARE PEACEFUL PEOPLE

It seems like we have moved from blessed to happy to prosperous and now we're looking at peace. If you've paid close attention, you will understand that at the center of the Psalm 112 lifestyle is peace—peace with God, which yields blessing, prosperity, increase, and peace with your fellow man. As Psalm 112 believers, we experience the blessing of God through His covenant of peace, or shalom.

The peace that we have at the center of the covenant blessings means that all our ways are governed by the peace of God. You will become protective of that peace because it insulates and protects you against the ups and downs of life. Peace leads you to make different decisions about your money, your career path, your relationships, and your family. Executing the judgments of a wise and discerning heart makes for peace. As the peace of God overtakes your life—prosperity increases, happiness increases, and your storehouse is full of the blessing of God—you will become a peacemaker. Your life will be governed by the question, "What makes for my peace?"

> Blessed are the peacemakers, for they shall be called the sons of God.
> —MATTHEW 5:9

> Blessed [happy, prosperous, and to be envied] are the peacemakers: for they shall be called the children of God.
> —MATTHEW 5:9, KJV

A child of God does not keep up a lot of confusion. A child of God is a peacemaker. Are you a peaceable person? Do you like mess? Prosperous people will walk away from a fight and confusion even if they don't get their point across. They see strife as detrimental to their prosperity. They do not make room for it in their lives.

You can disagree with somebody and still be peaceable. Contention is for the argumentative, the prideful, and those who have to have things go their way. Contention is for the double-minded. As a Psalm 112 believer, it does not belong in your life.

> If it is possible, as much as it depends on you, live peaceably with all men.
> —ROMANS 12:18

Pursue peace with all men, and the holiness without which no one will see the Lord.
—HEBREWS 12:14

He who would love life and see good days, let him keep his tongue from evil, and his lips from speaking deceit. Let him turn away from evil and do good; let him seek peace and pursue it.
—1 PETER 3:10–11

Sometimes we get so caught up in strife that we begin to think that it's normal to have problems. But it's not. You have the power to command good days in your life and to be at peace and full of blessing and prosperity. Some don't think they are living unless it's hard. But that is not why Jesus died. You can have a good life, especially when you keep your tongue from evil. Watch your mouth. Don't gossip. Don't argue. Don't fight. Don't stir up confusion. And don't keep company with people who take part in that behavior. Seek peace. Peace is prosperity. You cannot have prosperity if you don't control your tongue.

As a child of God filled with the Holy Spirit, confusion and strife should vex you and disagree with your spirit, because peace is a fruit of the Spirit (Gal. 5:22). You can't be around that. It is not normal.

There is, of course, a time for war and self-defense (Ps. 120:7), but as much as is possible, a prosperous person maintains a strict policy of peace. She knows the value of the blessing of God. She knows the price paid for peace, so she protects it. She protects the blessing of God. She protects her wealth and riches. She loves life, she promotes peace, and she sees good days.

OBTAINING THE PEACE OF GOD

When the world, which is always struggling to find peace, wants peace, where is the model? Whom can the world look at to see a model of peace? Where can the world find a group of people from all different backgrounds—black and white, Jew and Gentile—who come together and live in peace because of the Prince of Peace? There is only one place that this can truly happen—the church.

> Behold, how good and how pleasant it is for brothers to dwell together in unity!…for there the LORD has commanded the blessing, even life forever.
>
> —PSALM 133:1–3

God intended for His people to be a model of shalom to the world. This is why He highlights people like Job and the Psalm 112 man. He wants to show the world that there is a place where the lion lies down with the lamb (Isa. 11; Isa. 65). This is a picture that represents the coming of the Prince of Peace into the hearts of people whereby they can love people whom they once hated. You cannot be a child of God if you hate people (1 John 4:20). The church is the one place where we can show the world how to live in peace. That is our calling. But if you look around on Sunday morning, the picture isn't always so peaceful.

The church should be a community of peace, but it has been known to be like a war zone. I've been to churches where the deacons come to church with guns. I've heard of pastors setting guns on tables at meetings letting everyone there know that if things get crazy, they're ready for it. People post church fights on YouTube. And we've all been to board meetings where things turned bad. Listen, this is not *GoodFellas*; this is the church!

How is it that we can be in church and call ourselves children of God, and be full of the devil? It is because even believers need to experience the true shalom of God. We need a revelation of His covenant of peace that He fulfilled through His Son, the Prince of Peace, who came preaching the gospel of peace, the gospel of the kingdom. We need to repent of our unbelief in this area in order to receive it.

Some of us don't realize that we reject the peace of God by thinking and teaching that life should be hard or that God does not want us to be happy and prosperous. We reject the covenant of peace when we think all good things are on hold until Jesus comes again. When we are double-minded, we do not walk in the peace and prosperity of God. Double-mindedness causes us to reject the things of God even if we are saved.

When we are not aligned with God, when we don't have faith that He is our peace, we can pray for peace all year long, but without Jesus, who is the Prince of Peace, shalom will never come. This kind of thinking puts limits on God, who longs to bless His people. God hates being limited. There is no end and no limit to His peace. It is His desire to release it in every area of your life.

Peace comes to those who are the saints of God. Romans 1:7 says, "To all who are in Rome, beloved of God, called to be saints: Grace to you and peace [prosperity, shalom] from God our Father and the Lord Jesus Christ." Are you a saint? Are you grafted into the family of God? Are you the spiritual seed of Abraham?

As a saint of God, God wants you to renew your mind (Rom. 12:1–2) so that you can be like the Psalm

112 man—consistent, steadfast, and single-minded. You cannot be carnal and fleshly during the week—not reading and studying the Word, and not treating people right—then prophesy and speak in tongues when you get to church. You will not have peace and prosperity that way.

> To be carnally minded is death, but to be spiritually minded is life and peace, for the carnal mind is hostile toward God, for it is not subject to the law of God, nor indeed can it be, and those who are in the flesh cannot please God.
> —ROMANS 8:6–8

When your mind is governed by the Spirit of God, when you think like a saint, when you think good thoughts, when your mind is not controlled by your flesh, and when you meditate on the Word of God, you will have life and peace. You cannot be a carnally minded Christian and expect to have prosperity and peace.

Saints are spiritually minded. They are the holy ones. They are righteous. They fear God and delight in His commands. They carry the traits of the Psalm 112 man, who is uncompromisingly righteous. Can you say that this is who you are? It doesn't mean that you are perfect or don't make mistakes. It means that your lifestyle is holy and not sinful. Saints walk in a level of holiness that pleases God. They are not liars, drunkards, or whoremongers. They don't mistreat people. They live according to the Spirit of God. The verse above says that grace and peace come to those who are called to be saints. If you are a saint, prosperity and shalom belong to you. Romans 2:8–11 says:

> To those who are contentious and do not obey the truth, but obey unrighteousness, indignation, and wrath, will be tribulation and anguish, upon every soul of man who does evil, to the Jew first, and then to the Gentile. But glory, honor, and peace will be to every man who does good work—to the Jew first, and then to the Gentile, for there is no partiality with God.

Obedience, righteousness, and doing good work are our parts of the covenant that we must remain faithful to. Covenant is a twofold agreement. When we do our part, we have peace with God, and He makes even our enemies be at peace with us.

When a man's ways please the LORD, He makes
even his enemies to be at peace with him.
—PROVERBS 16:7

What has become like an enemy in your life? What
has the enemy come against—success, promotion,
health, relationships, marriage, children, or finances?
These are areas the enemy uses to keep us from believing God wants to see us happy, blessed, and prosperous.
He gets us off track with thinking we deserve to barely
get by, that God is mad at us, and that we should not
expect more and better. He keeps us bound by shame,
rejection, confusion, and condemnation. In some cases
we even blame God and get bitter at Him for the things
the enemy has done.

But I am here to tell you that the gospel of peace
is that Jesus Christ came and died so that you could
experience the shalom of God. The chastisement, or
price, of our peace was upon Him (Isa. 53:5). He was
beaten and crucified so you could have peace. If you
come under the rule of the Messiah, you can have peace.
You can have prosperity. You can live in safety. All the
evil beasts will be driven from your life. You will not
be tormented by devils. You will have the blessing of
God. This is the covenant of peace, and it belongs to
the saints of God.

Religion has conditioned us to believe that life should be full of trouble and that one day, by and by, we will go to heaven, and then we will have peace. The covenant of peace is not only for heaven but also for the here and now on earth. Your days should not be full of trouble. This doesn't mean that trouble will not come, but it does mean that you have the authority to stand up and tell trouble to go. You do not have to live a life of worry and anxiety. Peace is yours. Prosperity is yours.

The whole world is looking for peace, but there is only one way to peace and that is through Jesus. He says, "I am the way. I am Jehovah Shalom." Having Jesus in your heart is the way of peace, lasting joy, and abundant life. No Jesus, no peace, blessing, or prosperity. But you have a covenant of peace with God. God's covenant with His people from the beginning until now is what is at the center of the Psalm 112 promise. God wants to reveal this promise to you. He desires to bless you as He blessed the Psalm 112 man. He is there as a model of the faithfulness of the God who keeps His covenant.

DECLARATIONS FOR PEACE AND PROSPERITY

Shalom, prosperity, and peace are mine through Jesus Christ.

I am a saint of God.

I am a child of God.

I have a covenant with God.

My covenant is a covenant of peace, prosperity, and blessing.

I walk in covenant all the days of my life.

I enjoy shalom, prosperity, peace, and safety all the days of my life.

I will walk in covenant.

I will be faithful to the covenant through the blood of Jesus.

I have a covenant of shalom, peace, and prosperity in my life.

My life is good and my days are good because I keep my tongue from evil.

I hate evil, I do good, and I seek after peace.

I commit my life to peace and prosperity.

I will live in peace, I will walk in peace, and I will seek peace.

Jesus is my peace.

I am a peaceable person.

God is my Jehovah Shalom, my prosperity, and my peace.

I will walk in peace all the days of my life.

I will see good, I will love life, and I will have many good days.

I am blessed and I am prosperous because I am a peaceable person.

DECLARATIONS FOR A HAPPY AND BLESSED LIFE

I am happy because I fear the Lord.

I am happy because I delight in the law of the Lord.

I am happy because I have found wisdom and understanding.

I am happy because I receive the correction of God. I do not despise His instruction.

I am happy because I despise sin and have mercy on the poor.

I am happy because I handle matters wisely and trust in the Lord.

I am happy because my home is filled with children, both spiritual and natural. I am fruitful.

I am happy because I eat and enjoy the fruit of my labor. All is well with me.

I am happy because my God is the Lord.

I am happy because I have the God of Jacob for my help. My hope is in the Lord.

I am happy because I obey Your Word.

I am happy because the Lord has saved me. He is my shield and sword.

Chapter 3

GENERATIONAL BLESSING AND INCREASE

*His offspring shall be mighty in the land; the
generation of the upright shall be blessed.*
—PSALM 112:2

GODLINESS IN A person's life releases blessing upon the next generation and upon anything they birth or bring forth. When we think of generations and off-spring, we don't only need to think of what God will do for us in the natural, but we can also understand that God will bless us spiritually and in every area of our lives. If we want our seed—both natural and spiritual—to be blessed, we need to model our lives after the life of the man in Psalm 112.

The blessing of God brings increase, abundance, and multiplication into our lives. When I think about this second aspect of the promise of Psalm 112, I'm reminded of another favorite verse in a later psalm that says, "The LORD shall increase you more and more, you and your children" (Ps. 115:14). As believers who are working toward being established in God, we can begin to walk in this promise. Say this aloud: "The Lord shall increase me more and more, me and my children." This promise doesn't only apply to people with physical children, but it also represents anything that we are birthing. God wants to increase it. I call this kind of increase exponential increase that goes from generation to generation.

The first time the concept of blessing shows up in the Bible is when God blessed man and woman at the time of creation and said to them, "Be fruitful and multiply" (Gen. 1:28). God blessed them. Now there are seven billion people on the planet. Why? Because God blessed Adam and Eve and told them to be fruitful and multiply. Whatever God blesses increases. You cannot have the blessing of God and not increase.

Even after Adam and Eve fell and opened the door to sin and all kinds of evil, breaking covenant with God, He still found a way to bless and increase His people. Deuteronomy 30 talks about the blessings that come when we reenter God's covenant and keep His commands. He promises:

> Return to the LORD your God and obey His voice according to all that I am commanding you today, you and your children, with all your heart, and with all your soul.... The

LORD your God will bring you to the land which your fathers possessed, and you shall possess it. He will prosper you and multiply you more than your fathers.... The LORD your God will make you prosper in every work of your hand, in the offspring of your body, and in the offspring of your livestock, and in the produce of your land, for good.

—DEUTERONOMY 30:2–9

The blessing of God applies to everything we bring forth, from children to the work of our hands. This verse and the verses in Psalm 112 and 115 are written in the context of God's covenant with the house of Israel. God is a God of covenant. Everything that He has done for His people is by the provision of the covenant that He established at the foundation of the world. God's covenant of blessing is a thread that we can follow from Genesis to Revelation. This means that Israel is more than just a group of people whom God made a covenant with at Sinai. They are a continuation of God's effort to bless His children. Israel is also a type or picture of the body of Christ.

Now, of course, Israel rebelled, and we have too. But Jesus came to redeem us all. And through Him, we now have access to all the blessings of Israel. We have been grafted into the seed of Israel by the provision of the New Covenant. The promises of exponential increase and multiplication are for us and our children—if we are willing and obedient, and fixed and established in God. Increase extends to the whole kingdom of God. It is a kingdom concept. Even God's kingdom increases from generation to generation without end. (See Isaiah 9:7.)

GOD IS A GOD OF INCREASE

Again, anytime there is blessing, there will always be increase. And you need to have that mentality. Get delivered from a small mentality. Get an increase mentality. Growth, increase, and expansion are what God is about. We have to begin to look for the increase that comes with the blessing of God. Just thinking, "As long as I'm going to heaven," is not exponential thinking. That is not kingdom. That is not God. That is a mentality we need to break. If you can't handle increase, you can't handle God.

I remember years ago, when I first started preaching, I used to preach on the streets. I was saved at a street meeting. So I would go out into the streets, get my microphone, preach, and pass out tracts. We had a little team—my wife and some others. They would pass out tracts, and I would stand outside on the corner and preach. I didn't wait for a pulpit. I saw that I had a big pulpit out there. People would stop, we'd give them tracts, and then we'd lead them to the Lord.

I'll never forget: there was another guy out there preaching. He was one of those legalistic preachers. From his view, everybody was going to hell, including those in the church. He said that he knew the churches in the area weren't preaching the truth, because if they were, they wouldn't be packed and filled up. He believed that when you preach the truth, it will drive people away. He had a small and limited mentality that if you have increase, you can't be preaching the truth. He saw the truth as something that would make people mad and drive them away. He saw this as a holy and good thing. Having less meant your church is the pillar in the ground of truth and you're the only true church. He may have thought, "It's us four and no more. We are the only ones going to heaven. Our ladies' dresses are the right length, and our ladies don't wear pants. They don't wear makeup or jewelry. We don't chew tobacco, smoke, drink, or go to movies. We don't have fun. All we do is go to church, shout, dance, and wait for the Lord to come—and He's coming soon!"

This preacher was always right around the corner, preaching, "Time is almost winding up. We're living in the last and evil days. It's getting worse and worse. The devil is taking over, and demons are running the earth. It's getting worse. Wars and rumors of wars. Earthquakes and tsunamis. It's getting bad."

He didn't believe for increase because in his mind, it was all going to end in a few months anyway. He wasn't believing for people to get saved and for multitudes of believers to have financial increase, influence, and prosperity. He couldn't see that we have a promise that we will increase in power and in the glory of God. He wasn't believing for that. He saw that God's power and influence are going to decrease, and the devil is going to take over.

When people with this mind-set see increase, they say, "That can't be God." They don't have a mentality of increase. Their spirit doesn't even believe in increase. When increase comes, they get nervous. They can't handle it. It's too much. So for us to be ready to receive the increase, God has to do something inside of us. He has to break mind-sets that are small and limited. He has to give us a kingdom mentality. We talk about blessing, but with blessing comes increase.

DO YOU HAVE ROOM FOR MORE?

Like we see with the stable man of Psalm 112, God will increase you so much that you will not have room enough to receive it. (See Malachi 3:10.) The question is, Is your room too small? Do you need to make room for the blessing of God by breaking the religious mentality that you shouldn't have much? Isaiah 54:2–3 says:

> Enlarge the place of your tent, and let them stretch out the curtains of your habitations; spare not, lengthen your cords, and strengthen your stakes. For you shall spread out to the right hand and to the left, and your descendants shall inherit the nations.

God wants to do more for you and your descendants. He is able to do exceedingly abundantly above all that you could ever ask or think (Eph. 3:20), but you must make room.

Whatever you are thinking of now, God wants to do more than that. If God wants to do more, why would you stop Him? Why would you shortchange the blessing of God? We need to break free from this limited thinking and be satisfied and grateful for what God gives us—and He gives abundantly.

I remember years ago I attended a service when

someone got up and preached against prosperity, saying, "If God wanted you to be rich, you'd be born rich." This is the mind-set that many of us have, whether we realize it or not. This is a mind-set that we need to fight against.

BLESSED TO BE A BLESSING

When it comes to making room for God's increase, I am not talking about greed or covetousness. I am not talking about getting everything and hoarding it. We're not talking about selfishness. We're talking about being blessed to be a blessing. As we will see in later verses, the Psalm 112 man and his generations are blessed because he is generous and gives to the poor. He did not keep all of his wealth and riches for himself.

Just as God spoke to Abraham—"I will bless you and make your name great, so that you will be a blessing....and in you all families of the earth will be blessed" (Gen. 12:2–3)—He speaks to us. The blessing we receive as the seed of Abraham is designed by God to bless the whole world. God has called us and has given us life, light, revelation, and understanding. We are to take these gifts and be lights to the nations.

We have a covenant with God for peace, prosperity, blessing, deliverance, and increase. God's faithfulness to His covenant means that He will increase us and make us great, that His "blessings will come on you and overtake you if you listen to the voice of the LORD your God" (Deut. 28:2). He will make us the head and not the tail. We will be blessed coming in and blessed going out. We will be blessed in the city and in the field. Why? "Because you are My representatives," He says. "When the nations see what I have done with you, they will come running to you and say, 'Whoever your God is, I want to serve Him. What is your secret?'"

Blessed people share their secrets. They duplicate their efforts and philosophies. They share what they have because they know that generosity is a secret to prosperity. I'll share more on that in a later chapter. But for the purposes of seeing how living out your part of the Psalm 112 promise brings blessing to the people and things you physically or spiritually bring forth, I'll say this: passing on what you have to others is central to seeing increase come in every area of your life.

You see wealthy people share how they got to where they are when you turn on the television, watch a TED Talk, read a book, and so on. And they are eager to do it. It's hard to keep blessings a secret.

When you see someone who is doing well, wouldn't you welcome the opportunity to ask him, "What's your secret? Teach me. Train me." The Bible instructs us to do this as well when it comes to the ways of God. Think about this: If you had one hour to sit down with Solomon, what would you ask him? I hope you wouldn't ask him something like, "How does it feel to have seven hundred wives?" He was unstable and back-slidden at that point, but catch him on a better day and he would have some special insight about riches, success, and making good decisions, because God gave him wisdom to find his way to a place of influence and greatness. His father, King David, was a type of the Psalm 112 man, and we can see that God blessed Solomon, David's seed, and increased him more than any other king in the Bible.

If you had the chance to sit down with the wealthiest people alive in our time—Warren Buffett or Bill Gates, for example—what would you ask them? You wouldn't waste your time asking them what their favorite color is, or if they like catfish or perch. No, you would probably try to understand what is the key to their great success.

When God blesses someone, He elevates them. He uses them as a model so people who are still growing and learning can say, "There's a person," or, "There's a group. What is their key? Why are they so blessed?"

This is what God wants to do with us and our seed. He wants to multiply us because it attracts people. We become a blessing to others as we give them wisdom, knowledge, and understanding. We become a representative of God's love, blessing, and favor. We become a testimony that if God can do it for us, He will do it for others.

This is where the multiplication surpasses even natural bloodlines. This is where even our natural generations expand into the spiritual realm, and our fruitfulness brings children from all over the world, from every nation, kindred, tongue, and people. This is why this aspect of the Psalm 112 promise can apply to those who don't have biological children. Those who aren't married can have spiritual children and offspring whom the Lord will increase. We have to break out of the mind-set that limits our thinking even on this.

God is telling you to get ready, to enlarge the place of your tents, because your children are about to be multiplied because of the blessing of God on your life.

DON'T LIMIT PEOPLE'S ACCESS TO INCREASE

As we share through testimony or mentorship, or even as we respond to simple questions about how we got to where we are, our blessing and increase become a universal message that we can share with the world—from Africa to the Caribbean. I remember when I went to minister in Sudan. When I asked what I should speak about, the missionary hosts told me to just teach them to love their neighbors. Instead, I preached on the Holy Spirit. The power of God fell, and the people were filled and began speaking in tongues. It was amazing, but the missionaries had left the building in a panic over what had happened.

After the meeting and on our way back to where we were staying, I came to understand that the missionaries didn't think the teaching needed to be as full as it was. They had come to think that just a little bit of God was enough for the people. After all, they were just "pagans," just Africans.

I came with a different mind-set and wanted to release all that God had given to me to release to them. The blessing of the Holy Spirit was not too much for them. They had room for it.

It doesn't matter what color skin the person has, his nationality or ethnicity, or his family background; God can raise him up. When God gives you something to impart like blessings, wisdom, or revelation, don't hold it back from those who need what you have. Don't ever think you're up here and everybody else is down there, that they won't be able to handle the increase the Lord is about to release to them through you.

We have held on to all kinds of traditions that tell us

that God doesn't want us or the people to whom we are sent to impart blessing to have the fullness of His blessing. We limit their expectations of God by teaching them that to just have barely enough of His Spirit and everything else He brings is all God wants for them. Teach them the truth. Tradition will make the Word of God of no effect. But releasing what God has given you to the right people at the right time is how increase and blessing pass from generation to generation.

God wouldn't want to fill you to overflowing if He didn't want it to spill over into the lives of others. The Bible says that God "takes pleasure in the prosperity of His servant" (Ps. 35:27, AMP). If this weren't true, why did He raise up a Solomon? Why did He raise up a David? Why did He answer their prayers for success and prosperity? Why did He give them wisdom and favor? Why do we see from creation until this very day the thread of God's desire to bless and increase us and our children? Why did God answer the prayer of Jabez?

Jabez was mentioned in the Bible just so we could see the power of praying for increase and God's desire to answer that prayer. The Bible says:

> Now Jabez was more honorable than his brothers...Jabez called on the God of Israel, saying, "Oh, that You would indeed bless

me and enlarge my territory, that Your hand might be with me, and that You would keep me from evil, that it may not bring me hardship!" So God granted what he asked.

—1 CHRONICLES 4:9–10

That's it. That's all we ever hear about Jabez. He was honorable—a trait of a stable, steadfast, and established man—he prayed for blessing and enlargement, and God granted it to him.

We must break this mentality that just because we're saved, but see no increase, God is satisfied. Do you think God is pleased when there is no increase in your life? Do you think He is pleased when you don't increase in knowledge, wisdom, understanding, and revelation? Do you think God is pleased when you don't increase in power and increase in love? You don't increase in faith? You stay on the same level all your life? Do you think that pleases God? No.

You should be increasing in love, faith, power, revelation, and understanding. Your worship should be increasing. Your prayer should be increasing. Your ministry should be increasing. Your finances should be increasing. Your relationships should be increasing. There should always be more people being touched by your life.

Do you think God is satisfied when we stay on the same level and never grow? Do you think God is pleased when we are decreasing? No, He's not. God is a God of increase. God is pleased when we increase. God takes pleasure in increasing us. So His plan is, "the LORD shall increase you more and more, you and your children," (Ps. 115:14), and they will be mighty. (See Psalm 112:2.) Whatever comes out of you, God will increase. It will be mighty—strong, upright, brave— and blessed.[1]

YOUR SONS AND DAUGHTERS WILL INCREASE

God wants to increase your sons and daughters—and not just their physical, emotional, and spiritual wealth. He wants to increase them in number. Look back at Psalm 112:2. It says, "[Your] offspring shall be mighty in the land." Now look again at Isaiah 54:1: "Sing, O barren, you who did not bear a child. Break forth into singing and cry aloud, you who did not travail with child. For more are the children of the desolate than the children of the married wife."

The Lord has redeemed us. We were like the barren woman, unable to bear a child or a seed; we were not able to produce, multiply, or be fruitful until we came under the blessing of God. In returning to our covenant with God, He is saying that He will give us even more than the one who had been faithful. God wants to redeem the time that we were desolate and restore us quickly and abundantly.

He wants you to have more sons and daughters. You may have a few right now, but you will have sons and daughters around the world. This is about the blessing of God being released to all the nations of the earth. With business and ministry becoming global, it will be nothing for you to influence people in Asia or South America and teach them the ways of God, raising them up to expect God to do more for them—or for them to teach you and raise you up.

You may be reading this book and don't have children of your own. Maybe you volunteer with the youth in your church. Maybe you run a nonprofit organization that works in your community. Maybe you are on a team at work. All those to whom you are assigned are receiving an impartation of God's blessing through your life. This is how you increase and multiply.

AS YOU INCREASE, THEY INCREASE

God wants to give you the capacity to handle more sons and daughters. As you remain righteous and faithful to Him, He will not leave you on the same level. He has marked you for exponential increase. It is a law of the kingdom that in due season you will reap a harvest of blessing if you don't grow weary doing good. God's Word Translation says, don't allow yourself to "get tired of living the right way" (Gal. 6:9, GW). This is key to the Psalm 112 promise, as we will later uncover the stable man's righteousness continues or endures forever. He does not get tired of doing the right thing.

If you can look back over your life and see that God has helped you to remain faithful to Him and His Word, you should also be able to see that He has consistently been increasing you and all that concerns you.

You are not where you were five years ago. You have displayed a level of innovation that keeps you progressing, that keeps you getting better, stronger, and more plentiful. You are not living in the past. You are increasing. You know things now that you didn't know before. You've grown and increased in understanding. Your worship and knowledge of God has increased. Your level of discernment in ministry to others has increased. Your level of prophetic utterance and ability to hear from God and speak on His behalf has increased.

As a result, everyone and everything around you has benefited. Your children—both natural and spiritual—have become mighty and successful in the things they do at school, work, and home. Your marriage and other covenant relationships are thriving because you are increasing in love, kindness, and edification. The blessing and favor of the Lord has come upon your employer because you are there generously sharing your gifts and talents and working as unto the Lord. The people and groups of people to whom you minister are growing because you share your revelations from the Lord and the secrets to your success.

The Lord has enlarged you; therefore, they are enlarged. It's not enough just for you to increase; He wants to release exponential blessings, meaning blessings that are connected to your faithfulness and righteousness but that trickle down and extend to everything you have poured into. By demonstration, you are an expression of the kingdom of God. The kingdom doesn't stay on the same level. It keeps moving and progressing on every level, just as you are.

BREAK THE DESIRE
TO JUST MAINTAIN

What I have just described is a picture of God's plan for how the life of a stable, single-minded believer should be. This is not about perfection. If you look at the lives of King David and King Solomon, you will be able to identify the many times they failed. Laying claim to the Psalm 112 promise goes beyond relying on your own perfection; it is about relying on an accurate view of who God is. It is just as much about a mind-set and understanding as it is about the actions you take as a result of this knowledge. If there is any area of your life where you feel stuck—and I am not talking about times when the enemy is attacking or you are struggling in one season; we all struggle—if you struggle with old mind-sets and mentalities that keep you held back where you are not seeing growth, fruitfulness, and increase, you need a change of mind. This is what repentance is. Repentance leads you to admit your faults and seek the Lord for deliverance so that your life can produce and be fruitful.

I know there are times in a believer's life when the enemy seems to have come in like a flood. The believer's defenses are down. The gates have been torn down and his cities desolated. At this point, he is just trying to maintain to keep from losing everything. Increase is not on his mind. He needs deliverance from limiting and wrong mentalities.

Then there is the other kind of limitation that comes from being tired in the fight. As you increase, you are pushing against principalities, powers, and rulers of darkness who do not want to see the kingdom or its people advance. If you have been a believer for a while, you may have been delivered from your days as an un-believer, but now you may need to be delivered from a mind-set that just wants you to stay where you are. You just want to maintain a job. Promotion is not even in the picture. You don't want to deal with the stretch-ing that comes with growth. You got tired of warring, fighting, and breaking through.

Sometimes we don't want the increase of responsibil-ity that comes with larger territory. It's true: the more we get, the more responsibility we have. We cannot increase and have the same level of responsibility.

I have been there too, where I was in a maintaining mode. I just wanted to put it on cruise control. Relax. Take it easy. Retire. Don't increase. Don't grow. I've been there many times in my ministry. I said, "Look, I'm tired." Members would come to me and say, "Well, Pastor, we need to do this." I'd think to myself, "I'm not doing anything. Leave me alone. I'm tired. I'm just trying to keep this right here. I am just trying to hold steady." But then God challenged me, and I had to repent. I had to think about who He made me. I remember saying, "God, I'm not like this. I'm a pioneer. I'm an apostle. I can't just be a maintainer."

I've been to the nations. I've been on television. I've written books. More than one million copies of my books are in print in multiple languages around the world. But God said, "No, don't stop. Increase. I want to increase you more and more." I was challenged and provoked to action.

I pray that you are being recharged and challenged in this area. It's time for all of us to increase and go to another level of power, influence, authority, favor, grace, and blessing. It's time to increase—you and your children, you and your spiritual seed.

PEOPLE WHO CAN'T HANDLE INCREASE— THESE ARE NOT YOUR CHILDREN

There are those around you who are only interested in you as long as you maintain a certain level. They will not be able to handle this next level that God is taking you to. Some people can't handle increase. When God begins to bless your life, they get jealous. These are not your children; this is not your fruit. Their fear-filled and limited mentalities will cause them to reject the wisdom of God that will help them live in exponential increase.

There have been people like this in my life as well. Some would say, "Yeah, I remember when he didn't have anything." Then others would say, "Eckhardt, yeah, I remember Eckhardt. He used to work down there on Thirty-Ninth Street. I know Johnny. Yeah, he thinks he's something now." No, I know I'm something. I'm something in God. I don't think it; I know it. They would say, "He just left us." I sure did.

We can only be a blessing to others as much as they allow us to be a blessing. If they reject God, they are not ready to move with us to the next level, and we cannot stay back with them. This is how it was for Jacob when he was getting ready to leave after working in his uncle Laban's home for fourteen years. (See Genesis 31.) Laban knew Jacob had the blessing of God on his life, and Laban tried to hold on to Jacob because everything Jacob touched increased. Jacob had to sneak away because Laban wouldn't let him go. When Laban and his men came after Jacob, the Lord warned Laban to leave him alone. Jacob and Laban went their separate ways after making a peace treaty.

Joseph was another one who consistently increased and became the focus of his own brothers' jealousy and hatred. Even after he had been sold as a slave to another people, Joseph prospered. He had haters throughout his life. But no matter how much they tried to shut him down, lock him up, or put him in prison, they couldn't hold him back.

When increase and favor are on your life, it doesn't make any difference what people try to do to stop it.

What God has blessed, man cannot curse. No matter what others say or do, they cannot stop you from increasing and growing.

There is an anointing coming for increase, an anointing for exponential explosion and expansion. You're about to break out of that narrow place. That place is too small for you. You're going to break forth on the right hand and on the left. Your seed is going to inherit the Gentiles. There is something new coming upon you. You're going to have to add more room to get blessed, because now God commands increase on your life. Let God break you into another level of increase. It is time. You have maintained long enough. It's time for you to increase and go to another level of power, influence, authority, favor, grace, and blessing.

DECLARATIONS FOR GENERATIONAL BLESSING AND INCREASE

Lord, I declare that my children, my seed—both in the natural and spiritual—are mighty, strong, and successful in the earth. My generations are blessed and continually increasing.

Lord, I make room for increase. I believe that You take pleasure in my prosperity. I break any mind-sets and mentalities that cause me to think that You only want me to have just enough. You are the God of increase and the God of more than enough.

I break any traditional and religious mind-sets and mentalities that are set up to sabotage an increase in Your favor and blessing upon my life.

Increase everything I touch.

Increase me, and let me grow in every area.

Let my children increase. Don't let us stay on the same level. Lord, I want Your blessing on my life.

I break every limitation.

I break the demon of decrease, in Jesus's name.

I pray for exponential increase. I pray for more—more sons, more daughters, more children, more room, more blessing, more favor, more grace, and more finances.

I confess and decree increase in every area of my life— wisdom, revelation, knowledge, love, power, and anointing, in the name of Jesus.

I pray for an increase of finances, influence, power, ability, and grace for me and my children.

I declare that I will increase this year, next year, and the years to come. My ministry will increase. My business will increase. My worship and giving will increase. My nation will increase. My territory will increase. More and more and more.

Chapter 4

MORE THAN ENOUGH

Wealth and riches shall be in his house,
and his righteousness endures forever.
—Psalm 112:3

T HE PSALM 112 man is financially prosperous. He has more than enough. He is not consistently struggling with barely having enough to get by. He is living in the blessing of the Lord. The Bible says in Proverbs 10:22, "The blessing of the LORD makes rich, and He adds no sorrow with it." When you read Psalm 112, it gives insight into this man's character and heart. It helps us answer these questions: Why is this man blessed? Why are his children blessed? Why does this man walk in such a level of blessing? Is it accidental? Is it just for a few lucky people and not for others? Or is there something about this person's heart that causes him to prosper?

The secret is that this man knows whom he serves. He serves El Shaddai, the God of more than enough. As we discovered in the last chapter, God wants to increase us to overflowing with His Spirit and with His un-limited blessings. This includes financial abundance, what Psalm 112:3 calls wealth and riches. The Hebrew translation of the word *wealth* is "wealth, riches, sub-stances"; "enough, sufficiency."[1] It means "to possess riches," "to be in a position of ease."[2] *Riches* comes from a Hebrew word that means "to accumulate," "to pros-per," "to be happy," "to enrich."[3] In these translations and definitions, we find that both words are speaking of material possessions, resources, or provision. To have wealth and riches is to have more than enough material possessions, "to be in a position of ease."

Many of us get uncomfortable when we hear some-one say that the blessing of God includes material bless-ing and financial breakthrough. But according to the *International Standard Bible Encyclopedia*, "the pos-session of wealth is not regarded as sinful, but, on the contrary, was looked upon as a sign of the blessing of God (Eccles. 5:19; 6:2)."[4] So there is nothing to be un-comfortable about if you are wealthy and abide in Christ. There are certain kinds of sin wealthy people can be vulnerable to, as was the case with the rich young ruler in Luke 18:22–23. Pride is the most common trap for people of considerable means (1 Tim. 6:17) but also "oppression of the poor (James 2:6); selfishness (Luke

12 and 16); dishonesty (Luke 19:1–10); self-conceit (Prov. 28:11); self-trust (Prov. 18:11)."[5]

We can, however, use wealth wisely and bring glory and honor to the name of the Lord. This is what we see in the life of the Psalm 112 man. When we live holy, righteously, established in God, faithfully, obediently, generously, and wisely, our wealth pleases God and is a sign of His blessing on our lives.

This is why we must be mindful of the second part of this promise: "...and his righteousness endures forever." We will get to this in more depth later, but I want to be clear that this is not shallow prosperity teaching. This is not the kind of teaching that will tell you that all you have to do is have enough faith, speak it and declare it, and God will bless. That's only part of it. The other part is about what you do and how you live. Faith without works is dead (James 2:17). God gives wisdom, favor, blessing, opportunity, and divine power to us so we can get wealth (Deut. 8:18). Our acquisition of wealth confirms His covenant with us. So we play a big part in seeing the blessing of the Lord manifest in our lives. And it starts with our mind-sets.

As I have said, our minds need to be renewed and our expectations raised for what God has planned for us. We have to stop believing that wealth and abundance are something evil that God doesn't want us to have. When we misinterpret verses like "for the love of money is the root of all evil" (1 Tim. 6:10), we throw the baby out with the bathwater. This verse is not about remaining poor and needy and as a result becoming holier. This verse is about idolatry and covetousness or lust. Idolizing and lusting after money puts it in God's place as our source, which opens the door to all kinds of evil that comes as a result of selfishness and greed. This is where many of us have been trained to stop concerning understanding wealth. We put it all in one category under "evil" and something God doesn't want for us.

We need to pray for deliverance in this area, and this is the direction I feel the Lord wants me to take in these first few chapters. Before we can receive the full benefits of the Psalm 112 promise, we need to be in a position to receive and sustain them.

Wealth and riches are part of the covenant blessings of God. They are part of His plan for those who love and obey Him. His plans are good and not evil. He plans to prosper us and bring us to an expected end (Jer. 29:11, KJV). We need to understand and receive the truth that there are real benefits to walking in righteousness and in the wisdom of God. It is we who need to take the limitations off God and realize His blessing will overtake every area of our lives. Why would He increase us in every area except finances? There are no exceptions when it comes to the areas in which God will bless. Any kind of exception is man-made and a manifestation of our own limitations of what God will do.

In order for us to receive the promise of Psalm 112, we need to be set free to believe in an unlimited God who will bless us with more than enough.

GOD HATES LIMITATIONS

The Lord placed this message on being unlimited and breaking limitations in my spirit as I thought about the characteristics and mind-set of the Psalm 112 man. He had no problem with living right and being blessed. He had no problem with his faith. He saw that God would be faithful to His covenant as he remained faithful even through hard times. But many of us unknowingly limit God. There are times we are facing challenges in life and we forget the magnitude of His power. Psalm 78:41–43 says:

> Yes, they tested God over and over, and pro-
> voked ["limited," KJV] the Holy One of Israel.
> They did not remember His power, nor the
> day when He delivered them from the enemy,

how He had performed His signs in Egypt
and His wonders in the fields of Zoan.

As I was studying this passage of Scripture again
after many times before, I saw something interesting.
Not only did the people of Israel limit God, but God
was not pleased that they limited Him. Limiting God
will prevent you from having all that God wants for
you, and it displeases Him. It grieves Him and causes
Him to be upset. When you limit God, you're basically
saying, "God, I don't trust You to go beyond a certain
boundary or certain limit. I don't believe You can really
take me further than where I am or where I've been."
This kind of thinking is insulting to God because He is
all powerful. God is able to do exceedingly abundantly
above all that you can ask or think (Eph. 3:20).

Israel had God's track record right before them
and still did not believe Him. Their unbelief and dis-
obedience caused them to not be able to go into the
Promised Land and drive out the giants. An entire generation, except for Caleb and Joshua, died in the wilderness and did not enter the Promised Land because
they could not believe God could give them the ability to overcome those giants. (See Numbers 13–14.)
Psalm 78 reveals the four reasons some of us will not
get to live out the promise of Psalm 112: 1) we have

forgotten what He has done, 2) we don't believe, 3) we need deliverance from our past, and 4) we don't know God intimately. Let's take a closer look.

WE LIMIT GOD WHEN WE FORGET WHAT HE HAS DONE

The children of Israel did not have the faith to claim the promise of God because they had forgotten what He had done. But how do you forget signs, wonders, and miracles? How do you forget being miraculously freed from slavery? How can you even say that God is not able to bring us into the land when you saw the plagues God inflicted upon your enemies? How can you forget that God judged and destroyed the most powerful ruler of your time, that He parted the Red Sea, and that He provided manna in the wilderness and water out of a rock? How do you forget that God graced you with His presence in the form of a cloud by day and a pillar of fire by night? How do you doubt when you are part of a generation that saw some of the greatest miracles any generation has ever seen? How do you limit God just when it came time to cross over the Jordan and go into your possession of the land He promised to your forefathers?

It seems insane to be able to forget such supernatural

things, but remember Israel is a type and shadow. They are a cautionary example for believers in the New Covenant. So while this calls out their lack of faith and limiting God, it is also a picture of how we can do the same thing despite the overwhelming evidence of the contrary.

I believe that one of the reasons we are able to limit God is because we stop giving our testimony. Regularly talking about the great things God has done for you strengthens your faith and expectation for God to do great things for you in the future. The fact that you are even saved is a miracle. Think about what God delivered you from. God healed you and restored your mind. He performed signs and wonders while you were in Egypt (Egypt is a picture of the world). Think about, remember, rehearse, and recall how God brought you out, how He orchestrated your meeting the right people. Think about how God brought you into the Holy Spirit, the prophetic, the Word, and worship. Think about how God brought you into all the realms of the supernatural you are now walking in. Will you forget that? Or will all the great things God has done for you come rushing to your mind when you see the giants? When challenges come, will you say, "Oh, that's too big," and limit God because you forgot where God brought you from?

It's good to remember where God brought you from

and to rehearse what He has done for you. It's good to give your testimony as well. We don't have testimony services much anymore. But it is good to give your testimony to remind yourself and others that you are a miracle, that you are a sign and a wonder. Remind yourself and share with them that they are looking at someone who should be dead, if that's your story. It will strengthen you to stand in the midst of trouble and say, "No matter what is in my way and no matter how big it looks, I'm not going to limit God because if God did it for me then, He'll do it for me now. He's the same yesterday, today, and forever." Sharing your testimony will help you to remember that when it looked like it was impossible and there was no one to help you, God was there. You will be able to remember that even though you couldn't see your way and didn't know how you were going to get out of it, you are here because God came and rescued you.

Whatever is challenging you in your life right now— whether it's sickness, disease, or financial problems— whatever the mountain is, you can be like the Psalm 112 man and remember that God has you covered. He is more than enough. If it feels like you're stuck, can't get out of a rut, and just can't move, this is a good time to remember the God you serve is waiting to answer your cry for help. If it seems like things are not going well for you and you've lost your momentum and joy, remember a time when the joy of the Lord was your strength. If you've reached the place where you really can't seem to believe God to break through your circumstances— like the devil has set a barrier around you and says you can go no further, that you can prosper no more— remember the time when God showed His power strong on your behalf. The same God who brought you out years ago is here right now. As a matter of fact, He is not only here; He's already in your future.

GOD IS LOOKING TO BLESS THE ONE WHO BELIEVES

God does not like to be limited. He loves for people to believe. God enjoys when people take the limits off. The Bible says, "For the eyes of the LORD move about on all the earth to strengthen the heart that is completely toward Him" (2 Chron. 16:9). God is looking for somebody to believe in the strength and power of His might. He is searching the earth to find somebody who will believe Him for something bigger and greater. God will step over a billion people to get to you. God will bypass a billion people and stop at your house if while everyone else is doubting, you are the one who says, "I'm going to believe that God is able to do exceedingly abundantly above all that I could ask or think."

It's time to stop thinking small. It's time to stop limited thinking. It's time to stop being uncomfortable with the blessing and increase of the Lord. It's time to stop thinking that He will prosper you everywhere in your life except finances, except success and promotion. Psalm 112:3 says that wealth and riches shall be in your house if you are righteous. It's time to stop thinking that God will only take you so far and allow you to have so much. It's time to stop thinking that His blessing of wealth and riches only applies to a special group of people.

Let me tell you something—when you become a person of faith, you become one of God's special ones. When you become stable, steadfast, fixed, and established in God, you become one of the special ones. It's time to take the limits off.

With God nothing is impossible to you, and it's an insult when you tell God, "You can't do it. You can't bless me. You can't deliver me. You can't cause me to walk in favor." We're talking about God here, not man. We're talking about the God who can do anything, the God of all power, who performs miracles and turns things around overnight. We're talking about the

Creator of the universe, the One who made everything. How can you limit Him?

There have been times in my life when I have unknowingly limited God. I think all of us have. It's part of our process as we get to know who He is. I think that is why I like Psalm 112 so much. It is about a man who has come to know the power of God and has found peace in all matters of life because of the knowledge and fear of the Lord.

WHY WEALTH AND RICHES MAY BE HARD FOR YOU TO COME BY

This discussion about how we limit God is not to condemn you, because we all have fallen short, but to challenge you to get to know the character and ways of God. He is not slack concerning His promise (2 Pet. 3:9). He will be faithful to fulfill everything He has spoken. God is not a man that He should lie (Num. 23:19). If God said it, He's going to bring it to pass. But whether or not you are able to remain in the place He has brought you depends, again, on your mind-set.

Israel had been in bondage for four hundred years, and even though God had brought them out of bondage, the bondage was still inside of them. This is how it is for us. God can bring us out of something but unless

He gets *it* out of us, it will still manifest. That's why we need deliverance. Even after being liberated from Egypt, the Israelites were still full of fear and exhibiting the effects of the trauma they experienced while in bondage. When God spoke to them about taking possession of the Promised Land, they were not used to being people who owned anything. During those four hundred years in Egypt, they were not owners or people operating under their own volition. They were slaves. Slaves don't possess anything; slaves are the possession. So when God told them He wanted them to go in and possess the land of Canaan, He was speaking to a whole generation that had no context for taking ownership of anything. When they saw the giants, they said, "We can't do this."

If you are not used to possessing anything, when God says, "Possess. Take over. Wealth and riches are yours," you will have a hard time understanding what He is saying and how to accomplish it. When you've never owned a home, sometimes the hardest challenge is getting your first home. When you've never been to a certain level in life, and God says He wants to take you there, it's difficult.

People who possess things or are already rich have no problem getting more. They're used to having it. But for people who have never owned anything or had wealth, the blessing of God in this area can be hard to believe for and expect. Though the promises of God are equally yes and amen to all those in Christ (2 Cor. 1:20), taking possession of them may be harder for some than for others.

Your limitations are based on what you have come out of. Maybe you have been limited by society—there were certain places you couldn't go or certain things you couldn't do or have because of the color of your skin, family background, or economic situation. With deliverance, you can break through. You can declare that you are not going to remain limited by society or culture. No matter what your background is or how many people said you couldn't do it or have it, you don't have to be limited by any situation.

When you encounter God and He begins to work in your life, those limitations can be broken. The Bible says, "If any man is in Christ, he is a new creature. Old things have passed away. Look, all things have become new" (2 Cor. 5:17). As you come to Christ and hear the Word of God, you will also be connected to people of faith who will encourage you to break limitations. Soon you will be strengthened to know that you don't have to stay in a bound condition all your life. When you have God and people of faith around you, it won't matter how many haters and jealous people speak against the new place God is taking you. You will be able to declare, "I will not limit God!"

GOD DOESN'T BLESS EVERYONE

Now I'm going to write something that will challenge some religious thinking. Some people say that God likes and blesses everybody the same. He doesn't. God loves all people. God loves everybody. This is true, but God *likes* some people more than others. It's not because of them. It's not because of their flesh. The Bible says, "Jacob I have loved, but Esau I have hated" (Rom. 9:13). God didn't like Esau. It's messed up if God doesn't like you. I don't know about you, but I want God to like me. The Bible says that Abraham was the friend of God. God liked Abraham.

The thing that causes people to stand out in the eyes of God—just as the man in Psalm 112 stands out—is their faith. God does not like unbelief. He likes people who step out and dream and believe. God will do for those people what He cannot do for others who don't believe. God is no respecter of persons. God doesn't favor people based on their skin color, family name, or background, but He does delight in people who believe.

When you look at the New Testament during Jesus's ministry, the group of people whom you would think

He would have favored, He didn't. He only spoke favorably of the people who had great faith—and they were all Gentiles. They weren't Jews, His chosen people. When the centurion in Luke 7 came and said, "Lord, You don't even have to go to my house. Just speak the word" (see verses 6–7), the Lord said, "I tell you, I have not found such great faith even in Israel" (v. 9).

Sometimes the people we think should be breaking through don't because they are the very ones who limit God. And the people who are the most unlikely do break through because they think and dream big, knowing that if God says the word, it's done. Think about the Canaanite woman in Matthew 15 who came to Jesus because her daughter was possessed by a demon. Jesus ignored her at first. When He finally answered, it seemed like He insulted her: "I was sent only to the lost sheep of the house of Israel.... It is not fair to take the children's bread and to throw it to dogs" (vv. 24–26). Hearing a response like this, most of us would have turned around and walked away. But she pressed in and said, "Yes, Lord, yet even dogs eat the crumbs that fall from their masters' table" (v. 27). I can imagine Jesus thinking to Himself, "Oh, this is a bad girl here. I have to give her this miracle." She knew that even a crumb, a small piece of the anointing of the Lord would bring deliverance for her daughter. She was not going to be held back from the miracle she needed.

People may look down on you and call you a dog. They may tell you you're not worthy or you're not good enough. They may think you don't qualify. But if you have faith, you can receive your miracle. God likes people who have faith, because faith says that you know God. When you have faith, you are saying, "God, I trust You. I know You're able to do it." God likes that. It shows that you know Him and what His heart is toward people. He is a good, merciful, kind, forgiving, redeeming, delivering, and restoring God. He is the God who doesn't give us what we deserve. The people who really know God—that He is good and His mercy endures forever—those are the ones He favors.

Some of the most religious people don't even know God. With all the religious people in Israel, the Pharisees and Sadducees, Jesus singled out the Gentiles as the ones who had great faith. The religious leaders didn't know God. They went to theological schools. They sat at the feet of rabbis. They were taught the Torah and the Law—they could even quote it word for word—but they didn't know God.

I see this same thing among believers today. We don't even know what we have. People come in from the outside and get a miracle because they don't have all the religious baggage that clouds their ability to see how great God is. They don't limit Him.

I want to challenge you with this message from Psalm 112. I want you to know that with knowing God and walking in His ways comes a measure of blessing you have never seen before. We have been limited by what other people tell us about what God will do rather than claiming the full spectrum of the promises He has made to us. The abundant life is not only reserved for the sweet by and by. It is for us to claim right now.

I want you to see that both natural and spiritual wealth and riches are for you now. I challenge you with this word: Break the limitations off who you can be, where you can go, or what you can do. For your ministry, finances, business, family, or whatever it is, begin to believe God for miracles. Believe that He will do what He said He would do. Believe that He wants to bless you. Believe that He is more than enough. Be a person of great faith. Be the person God loves to bless. This is the heritage and legacy of a Psalm 112 believer. This is the life of a stable and steadfast man or woman of God.

As you take hold of this message and take the limits off of what God wants to do in your life, I believe that you will move into a season where you're going to see breakthroughs like you've never seen. You don't have to know how it's going to happen or where it's going to come from. All you will know is that your God is unlimited. He is great and powerful. He has an unlimited supply.

DECLARATIONS OF FAITH IN AN UNLIMITED GOD

Lord, You are unlimited. You are too great and too powerful for me to put limits on You. I will not insult You by limiting in any way what You desire to move in my life.

Lord, forgive me if I have limited You. Renew my mind and deliver me from wrong mind-sets and limited thinking.

I break through limitations in the name of Jesus.

Lord, I believe that You are able to do exceedingly abundantly above all I can ask or think.

I will live a life that is unlimited.

I declare that every time it looks like I have come to a limit, God is going to take me further. Every time it looks like I have hit a wall, I will believe when God says the wall is coming down. Every time it looks like I can't go any further, I will believe when God says I am stepping over into something new.

This is my season for wealth and riches to dwell in my house. This is my season to be overtaken by the blessings of God. This is my season to walk in righteousness and wisdom.

I walk in a new realm of unlimited favor, unlimited breakthroughs, and unlimited resources.

I will not be held back by unbelief. I will not be held back by my past. I will not be held back by people.

I take possession of the prosperity God has for me. I am in position to receive it and to walk in it continuously.

I serve an unlimited God. I serve the God of more than enough.

Thank You, Lord, for breaking every limitation in my life, in Jesus's name.

Chapter 5

GRACIOUS AND COMPASSIONATE

*To the upright there arises light in
the darkness; he is gracious, and full
of compassion, and righteous.*
—Psalm 112:4

In CHAPTERS 2 and 3 we looked at the overall picture of the blessings God promises to you as a Psalm 112 believer. In this chapter and the next several to follow, I am going to highlight some of the character traits that open the door to these blessings and cause them to remain in your life.

As I said, our ability to prosper and receive the promises of God has to do with our renewed hearts and minds. We prosper first on the inside before our prosperity manifests on the outside. As the apostle John said, "Beloved, I pray that you may prosper in all things and be in health, just as your soul prospers" (3 John 2, NKJV). Man is a triune being. We are made of body, soul, and spirit. What happens in our hearts and minds—mental and emotional states—is the soul realm. How much you prosper physically, spiritually, emotionally, relationally, and financially depends on the condition of your soul. Out of the soul flows either the fruit of the Spirit or the works of the flesh. (See Galatians 5:19–23.) Our souls display the fruit of the Spirit when our souls come under the control of the Spirit of God. He gains access to us through our spirits. Proverbs 20:27 says, "The spirit (conscience) of man is the lamp of the LORD, searching and examining all the innermost parts of his being" (AMP). And in Romans 8:14–16 we read, "For as many as are led by the Spirit of God, these are the sons of God.... The Spirit Himself bears witness with our spirits that we are the children of God."

THE PSALM 112 MAN LIVES BY THE FRUIT OF THE SPIRIT

The first two character traits we come across in Psalm 112 are grace and compassion. It's interesting that these relate to how the Psalm 112 man treats other people. The first three verses talk about how he relates to God and the blessings that come as a result of honoring that relationship. In fact, the whole psalm alternates, verse by verse, between our relationship with God and our relationships with others. It brings to mind what

Jesus called the greatest commandments, which are to love God and to love others as we love ourselves. (See Matthew 22:37–39.)

Being able to love God and love people has everything to do with the position of our hearts. In the New Covenant, we've come to see these as abilities that can only come as a result of being filled with the Spirit of God. Empowered by Him, we are able to be gracious, compassionate, and righteous, which categorically relates to the fruit of the Spirit. The nine fruit—love, joy, peace, patience (even temper), gentleness (or kindness), goodness (benevolence), faith (or faithfulness), meekness (also gentleness and humility), and self-control—can be summed up in how the Psalm 112 man displays grace, compassion, and righteousness. A breakdown of the meaning of these three words shows us the connection to the fruit of the Spirit.

Grace

Merriam-Webster's dictionary defines *grace* as a "disposition to or an act or instance of kindness, courtesy, or clemency"; "the quality or state of being considerate or thoughtful."[1] Also, the traits benevolence, courtesy, kindness, mercy, virtue, excellence, merit, and charity are related to grace and graciousness.

Compassion

Compassion is related to mercy[2] and is defined as "sympathetic consciousness of others' distress together with a desire to alleviate it."[3] It is also connected to empathy, kindheartedness, mercy, sensitivity, benevolence, generosity, goodwill, largeheartedness, and philanthropy.[4] When used in the Bible, compassion is seen as a trait that can only come from God.[5]

Righteousness

Righteous means just, lawful, right (in one's conduct), correct.[6] It is also connected to decency, goodness, honesty, integrity, morality, uprightness, virtue, honor, respectability, and faithfulness to high moral standards.[7] Righteousness is a trait that shows up several times throughout Psalm 112, but I will come back to explore it in greater depth in a later chapter.

Looking at these three traits listed in Psalm 112:4, we can see how they cross-relate to the fruit of the Spirit. These traits are demonstrated by a person who walks according to the Spirit of God, not a person subjected to his or her flesh.

THE DOUBLE-MINDED CANNOT
LIVE ACCORDING TO PSALM 112

When you are bound by double-mindedness—rejection, rebellion, and bitterness—you cannot also be gracious, compassionate, and righteous.

A double-minded person is usually one who was rejected by people very early in life and becomes rebellious. Oftentimes, when a child becomes very rebellious, it is a cry for attention because he or she feels rejected. Also, when people have been rejected, they struggle with forgiving those who have hurt or rejected them and they become bitter.

No one likes to be rejected. Being rejected is one of the most painful things that can happen to you. You can say it doesn't bother you, but rejection will always bother you. You may become bitter, angry, unforgiving, retaliatory, resentful, and hateful. These characteristics cannot dwell within the heart of the Psalm 112 believer alongside graciousness and compassion. As it says in James 3:11, no spring can yield both salt and fresh water.

Psalm 112 believers are not judgmental, legalistic, cruel, vindictive, or bitter. When they deal with people, they are gracious, kind, and loving. You cannot be this way as a double-minded person. Your rejection, anger, rebellion, and bitterness will eventually come out.

The way to get rid of these dangerous and fleshly traits and become a believer who lives according to the Psalm 112 life is deliverance—being set free to live a Spirit-filled life.

Psalm 112 believers prosper because their souls have been delivered. They display the fruit of the Spirit because their souls have been renewed and transformed. They have placed them under the control of the Spirit of God. Their souls don't rule them; the Spirit does. The Spirit has placed within them the power and fortitude to prosper in every area of life, from the inside out.

THE WORKS OF THE FLESH
ARE PROSPERITY THIEVES

Bitterness, anger, unforgiveness, and other works of the flesh are prosperity thieves, demons and devils that keep you connected to your past and rob you of your future. But God wants to break you from that link of a painful past so you can move forward into the prosperous plans He has for you.

We must pray and ask God to show us any hidden or repressed memories of events in our lives that are causing bitterness. There is something called memory recall or flashback that people suffer from or deal with. This is when a person remembers every bad thing that has happened to them, everything that someone has done to them. They tend to remember these things and store them up, and this often comes out when the person does the same thing to them again. That action reminds them of what had been done to them in the past.

When God forgives us, He puts our sins in the sea of forgetfulness, or the depths of the sea (Mic. 7:19). He forgets them. He doesn't remind us of them. This is what healing from God in these areas will empower us to do. This doesn't mean that you will forget the events entirely; it just means that when you recall them, you will not feel that same pain, hurt, and anger you felt before you truly forgave and let things go. You don't want things in your past to prevent you from moving into your future.

It can be hard to imagine living a life of consistent kindness and compassion because of how many knuckleheads, fools, idiots, or selfish and abusive people you come up against in life. Rest assured that the Psalm 112 man came across many idiots in his life. Sinful, wicked, and ungodly people will do and say things with no regard for anyone else. There will always be people like this in the world—we meet them all the time—but there is a clear distinction in how Psalm 112 believers will conduct themselves.

The idea of fighting fire with fire is not OK for a believer. Never allow yourself to become like them, because you want the blessing of God on your life. You want to always be kind, courteous, gentle, loving, considerate, and godly. This is what God expects of you. He expects His saints to have a godly standard. You cannot allow your reactions to the trials and trauma of life to steal God's blessing from you.

The secret to staying faithful to God and maintaining a heart of grace and compassion is to be yielded to the Spirit of God.

WALKING IN THE SPIRIT

When we talk about the characteristics of Psalm 112 believers, we're actually talking about the lifestyles of people who are led by the Holy Spirit. They follow the Spirit of God and do not walk in the flesh. When you are led by your flesh, your flesh dominates you, so you are not led by your spirit. Your spirit is not alive. It is not filled with the Holy Spirit. It is dead to the things of God. You are controlled by your flesh.

When you are born again and your spirit comes alive, the Holy Spirit comes into your spirit and now your spirit is to take control of your soul—your flesh. But your flesh, having once been in charge, does not like to give up control easily. Now that you are born again, filled with the Spirit of God, and beginning to walk according to the fruit of the Spirit, your flesh doesn't quite understand: "Why can't I fornicate anymore? Why can't I do that? Why can't I hate people anymore? Why can't I get drunk anymore? What happened?" Your spirit has come alive is what happened. God is a Spirit, He dwells in your spirit, and now your spirit has become the ruler of your life.

The trouble that some of us have is when things from our past such as rejection put up a fight for control. Demonic spirits fight for control over our flesh to keep it in a place of power over our spirits. This is where we get the wavering and double-minded behavior so commonly experienced. But our flesh was always meant to be under the rulership of our spirits. This is the way to the fixed, established, and prosperous life we see in Psalm 112. This man is not ruled by his flesh.

In order to dethrone the flesh for good, get delivered, yes. But there is also the process that Paul talks about: "I discipline my body and bring it into subjection" (1 Cor. 9:27, NKJV). The New Living Translation uses the word *training*. Paul said he did this so that he would not be disqualified or "unfit [not stand the test, be unapproved and rejected as a counterfeit]" (AMP). Paul desired to be approved and accepted by God more than anything, and he knew God had a standard that went against the natural grain of Paul's sinful flesh.

As Paul taught, we have to train our flesh—our bodies—and bring it under subjection to the Spirit of God, because most of our behavior is habitual. We generally do the same things over and over again without even thinking about it. A lot of what we do is subconscious. We can do something so long that it becomes second nature like brushing our teeth when we first get up in the morning or driving home from work. Have you ever been driving home from work and realized you weren't even thinking about where you were going? You just showed up at home. We do many things like this subconsciously. We don't have to think about them.

Sometimes the things we do without thinking are sinful. Habitual sins are sometimes the hardest to break. They can form strongholds in our lives. I've referred to some of them as "stubborn demons" in my books *Deliverance and Spiritual Warfare Manual* and *God's Covenant With You for Deliverance and Freedom*. This kind of demon often doesn't come out except through fasting and prayer, which is part of the spiritual discipline and training Paul was talking about. With fasting, you weaken the flesh and strengthen the spirit. Over the course of my ministry and in my own life, I have discovered that this is true: if you change your habits, you will change your life.

WALKING IN THE SPIRIT CHANGES HOW YOU TREAT PEOPLE

Often when we talk about being Spirit-filled, we talk about power, anointing, singing, prophesying, and speaking in tongues. All of that is good, but grace, compassion, kindness, love, and gentleness toward others are also manifestations of being Spirit-filled. Don't tell me you're Spirit-filled when you are mean, hateful, and evil, but you speak in tongues. If you are filled with the Spirit of God, you should display God's main characteristic—love.

We can't say that we love God and hate people. According to 1 John 4:20, you are a liar if this is how you live. People who are filled with God's Spirit and have control over their flesh are filled with and display the love of God toward others.

The first fruit of the Spirit is love. You can love people despite what they are doing. Yes, some people need deliverance, but love covers a multitude of sins (1 Pet. 4:8). Love endures all things (1 Cor. 13:7). If you can't love people but you can shout and dance, you will not make it for long because the devil will set you up to get hurt and angry. He will cause you to walk right into the trap of rejection and bitterness. The love of God shields you from bitterness. It helps you to endure the faults and failings of other people.

There is not a person who has been saved for any period of time who has not had to deal with something somebody said or did. As I said before, in this life you will deal with knuckleheads, fools, and idiots. You need to train your flesh to be submitted to love so that you can endure, so that you will not be disqualified and unfit to receive the blessings and promises of God, so that your life will be full of joy, peace, and righteousness in the Holy Spirit.

This is not about maintaining close ties with sinful or unhealthy people or letting destructive people remain in your life. That is not wise. Love does not rejoice in evil, unrighteousness, sin, or injustice (1 Cor. 13:6). But what we are talking about is extending the love, mercy, and compassion of God. There are times when you have to just overlook what some people do. You have to let their actions roll off your back. You can't pay it attention. Some older saints may tell you, "Just say, 'God bless you,' and go on about your way."

HOW TO WALK IN THE SPIRIT

For many of us, being able to consistently show love, grace, and compassion, especially to difficult people or in difficult circumstances, is where we need to be strengthened. In Jude 18–21, we find the way to do it:

> "In the last days there will be scoffers who will walk after their own ungodly desires." These are the men who cause divisions, sensual, devoid of the Spirit.
>
> But you, beloved, build yourselves up in your most holy faith. Pray in the Holy Spirit. Keep yourselves in the love of God while you are waiting for the mercy of our Lord Jesus Christ, which leads to eternal life.

In other words, you are going to come across difficult people who are divisive and devoid of the Spirit. But to deal with them and remain in Christ, there are three things you need to do:

1. Build yourself up

Receive the Holy Spirit. Get delivered. Read and study the Word. Fast and pray. These are the ways that you can begin to see an increase of the Spirit of God operating in your life. When you build up your spirit to receive the fullness of God's Spirit, you break the grip of the enemy off your life and you are able to access the power of God without any hindrances. You can't live the Psalm 112 life without the power of God. The Bible says that "you shall receive power when the Holy Spirit comes upon you" (Acts 1:8). It is not by might nor by power but by God's Spirit that we will be built up and strengthened to live a life of grace and compassion toward others. Trying to live this without the power of the Holy Ghost will land you in a hospital. God never intended you to try and serve Him in the energy of your flesh. He said, "I'm going to give you a helper who will teach you all things." (See John 14:26.)

2. Pray in the Holy Spirit

Praying in the Holy Spirit is one of the keys to walking in the Spirit. The phrase refers to the times when the Holy Spirit prays through us the perfect will of God. Romans 8:26–27 says, "Likewise, the Spirit helps us in our weaknesses, for we do not know what to pray for as we ought, but the Spirit Himself intercedes for us with groanings too deep for words. He who searches the hearts knows what the mind of the Spirit is, because He intercedes for the saints according to the will of God."

Praying in tongues strengthens your spirit and helps

you get control of your flesh. It reduces fleshly reactions and causes you to react out of your spirit instead. Paul, one of the leading apostles in the New Testament church, said, "I thank my God that I speak in tongues more than you all" (1 Cor. 14:18). He said this because of all the people issues he had to deal with throughout his ministry. He couldn't afford to react out of his flesh, lest he risk the effectiveness of the gospel he preached.

You can speak, pray, and sing in tongues. Ephesians 5:18–19 says, "Be filled with the Spirit. Speak to one another in psalms, hymns, and spiritual songs, singing and making melody in your heart to the Lord." In other words, other ways to stay filled with the Holy Spirit are to spend time worshipping and singing prophetic songs.

As you increase your private devotional time and include praying and singing in the Spirit, you will begin to see changes in your life and the way you see and deal with people. You will be more sensitive to the Holy Spirit, hearing His voice and being led by Him. Your thoughts, judgments, and prayers for others will change. There is only so much we can see about others through our limited and fleshly perspective. Praying in the Spirit opens us up to God's unlimited understanding of everything that is happening in all of our lives. As you see people through the Spirit, you will be filled with God's love and mercy. You will not be so quick to snap and lash out at them because you will see where they hurt. You will also be humble enough to recognize that without the grace and compassion God has shown you, you might be in worse circumstances than they are. You will have compassion enough to say that while they may not be living right or responding right, God has the power to turn their lives around just like He did yours.

3. Keep yourself

From the Book of James we learn that the tongue is the part of your body that controls your whole life. If you can keep or control your tongue, you can keep yourself and control your life. Psalm 112 believers are a Spirit-filled people whose lives are under control. They are not out of control. They keep their tongues from speaking whatever the flesh drags up; therefore, they keep themselves under control and in the love of God.

In comparing the tongue to the small rudders that steer large ships or the bit in a horse's mouth that controls its whole body, James said:

> See how we put bits in the mouths of horses that they may obey us, and we control their whole bodies. And observe ships. Though they are so great and are driven by fierce

winds, yet they are directed with a very small rudder wherever the captain pleases. Even so, the tongue is a little part of the body and boasts great things. See how great a forest a little fire kindles. The tongue is a fire, a world of evil.

—James 3:3–6

It is for this reason that one of the first things that happens when you get baptized in the Holy Spirit is that He gets a hold of your tongue. If the Spirit of God begins to control your tongue, He will be able to direct your life and bring you into agreement with God. You will begin to see supernatural things happen in your life and in the lives of those you impact through prayer and ministry. Miracles, healing, and deliverance will come into situations that seemed impossible. God will do for you exceedingly abundantly beyond all that you ask or imagine, according to the power of God working in you. (See Ephesians 3:20.)

Your tongue is very important. It's important to yield it to the Holy Spirit. It's important that what you say is correct. Proverbs 18:21 says, "Death and life are in the power of the tongue." We know that one of the reasons people are messed up in their lives is because they have not controlled their tongues. They have not controlled what they have said. They have allowed their tongues to speak things from their hearts that are incorrect, ungodly things that bring destruction into their lives.

I encourage you to pray in the Holy Spirit. Speak in the Spirit. Live in the Spirit. Move in the Spirit. When you put yourself under the control of the Spirit of God, He will lead you to a life that will manifest the Psalm 112 promise. Your grace and compassion to others will bring shalom into your life.

PRAYERS FOR WALKING IN THE SPIRIT

Heavenly Father, I thank You for the power of the Holy Ghost.

I yield my life, my tongue, my mind, and my body to the power of the Holy Ghost.

I will not walk in the flesh. I will not live in the flesh. I will live in the Spirit. I will walk by the power of the Holy Ghost.

Lord, I submit myself to Your Holy Spirit.

Holy Spirit, I give You permission to lead me, guide me, and empower me. I submit my life to You.

I will walk in the Spirit. I will have the fruit of the Spirit: love, joy, peace, gentleness, long-suffering, kindness, meekness, and temperance.

I thank You, Lord, that as I walk in the Spirit, Your fruit will be the manifestation of my life.

Thank You, Lord, for the fruit of the Spirit increasing in my life.

Because of Your Spirit, I have grace and compassion for others. I keep myself in the love of God.

Because of Your Spirit, I am able to see people through Your eyes and love them with the love of God.

Thank You, Lord, for the Holy Ghost. I am a spiritual person. I am not fleshly. I am not carnal. I am not dominated by my flesh. I renounce all the works of the flesh in the name of Jesus.

My flesh will not dominate and rule my life, but I will be led and controlled by the Holy Spirit all the days of my life. In Jesus's name, amen.

Chapter 6

WISE AND JUST

A good man deals graciously and lends; he will guide his affairs with discretion ["justice," AMP and MEV].
—PSALM 112:5, NKJV

THE NEXT VERSE in Psalm 112 deals again with grace, generosity, and discretion. We dealt with the grace and compassion of the Psalm 112 man in the last chapter and discussed how they flow out of a life submitted to the Spirit of God. His generosity is a recurring theme, like his righteousness, and I will explore both in later chapters. In this chapter I want to focus on how he conducts the affairs of his life with discretion.

The word *discretion* refers to judgment, decision-making; how a process or manner of deciding what should be done is carried out—proper, fitting, right.[1] It also means "the quality of having or showing discernment or good judgment"; "ability to make responsible decisions."[2] People who operate with discretion have common sense. They are levelheaded, prudent, sensible, astute, insightful, and wise. They think things through. They exercise caution. They plan things out in advance and logically consider the available options. They are not guided by emotions or coercion. They are disciplined and exhibit self-control.

Other Bible translations say that the Psalm 112 man conducts his business fairly (NLT) or with justice (AMP and MEV). I like the word *discretion* because it includes those ideas but gives greater depth to the way this man lives his life.

Good judgment, responsible decision-making, insight, and prudence are more character traits we should seek to emulate in our lives as we learn to live the Psalm 112 promise, and all of them fall under the spirit of wisdom.

WISDOM IS THE PRINCIPAL THING

Psalm 35:27 says that the Lord "[takes] pleasure in the prosperity of His servant" (NKJV). I mentioned this verse earlier, and I may quote it again later, because we need to break the mentality that God doesn't want to see us prosper. God is delighted when we as His servants prosper. I made it a point to memorize this verse years ago to remind myself that not only does God want us to prosper, but He also takes great pleasure in it. God gives us power to get wealth so that He may establish His covenant (Deut. 8:18). He also said to Joshua, "Meditate on [My Word] day and night so that you may act carefully according to all that is written in it. For then you will make your way successful, and you will be wise." God doesn't just give us prosperity; He gives us power (strength, might, ability[3]) to get it, which comes in different ways and they all start with wisdom. We see that this is how God manifested His covenant in the life of the Psalm 112 man.

When you talk about prospering in life, you are talking about success. Wisdom is a key to success. But with all the teaching on prosperity, wealth, blessings, and riches, very seldom have I heard it taught in connection to wisdom. Most often it is taught that prosperity can come by a miracle from God, through supernatural breakthrough, from giving, or through the Word, and I believe in all of that. I teach and preach it. But prosperity—riches and honor—comes to and stays with the person who is wise. This is why I recommend studying Psalm 112 with Proverbs, especially Proverbs 8. This passage of Scripture is another one of my favorites that I read over and over again. It teaches the value and importance of wisdom.

Proverbs 4:7 says, "Wisdom is the principal thing" (KJV). You ought to memorize this verse as well. Notice that it doesn't say faith is the principal thing; it doesn't even say love is the principal thing, even though you need both of them. It says wisdom is the principal thing. If you are going to live your life, you must first have wisdom.

The man in Psalm 112 is noted for his wise dealings in all of his affairs. If we are to experience a prosperous life as he did, we too must have wisdom as a guiding force in our lives. Let's take a look at some of the main verses in Proverbs 8 to learn what it means to live wisely—with discretion and justice leading everything we do.

HOW WISDOM WILL
LEAD YOU TO A GOOD LIFE

There is so much foolishness in the world today. Many people do not understand that getting wisdom needs to be a priority. It is the chief thing, the most important, foundational, and basic thing you need if you are going to prosper. You cannot get ahead by listening to and applying foolishness. Foolishness leads to misery, bitterness, confusion, instability, and poverty. But if you cherish, love, and seek after wisdom, you will live a good and happy life. Here's how:

Wisdom gives good advice

> Counsel is mine, and sound wisdom; I am
> understanding, I have strength.
> —Proverbs 8:14

Wisdom gives you understanding to discern the things of God and the things of the Spirit. It helps you to discern what is good counsel and what direction to follow. Wisdom gives you this strength (power, might, ability), which is the same strength that gives you the power to determine the way to wealth, prosperity, and success.

Wisdom makes way for you to rule and reign

> By me kings reign, and princes decree justice.
> By me princes rule, and nobles, even all the
> judges of the earth.
> —Proverbs 8:15–16

Because everything that was a shadow in the Old Testament has been made full and complete through the New Covenant, we know that we—man or woman—are the kings, princes, nobles, and judges this verse speaks of. Ephesians 2:6 says, "[God] raised us up and seated us together in the heavenly places in Christ Jesus." Then 1 Peter 2:9 says, "You are a chosen race, a royal priesthood, a holy nation, a people for God's own possession."

It has been God's plan from the beginning for us to rule and reign with Him. *Reign* means "to be or become king or queen," "to be made king or queen." It is closely related to *rule* and *govern*. It also means to counsel, advise, or consider.[4] *Rule* means to contend, have power, prevail over, exercise (a right), to get, and to have dominion.[5]

This is the place from which our lives were meant to be lived, and it is God's wisdom that brings us back to this place. Life should not just be happening to us. The enemy should not be allowed in and out of our lives anytime he wants. God's wisdom gives us governing powers over the territory He has given us, whether it's our family, business, or ministry. Wisdom brings us back to the place where we are governing our lives, where we are not living passively and being overtaken by the enemy, and where we prevail and have power over the direction of our lives. This is the dominion God created us for. (See Genesis 1:26.)

If you want to live like this, get wisdom.

Wisdom makes itself easy to find

> I love those who love me, and those who seek
> me early will find me.
> —PROVERBS 8:17

Some take the word *early* in this verse to mean early in the day, in the morning, or at dawn. They take it to mean that we should seek wisdom first thing in the morning. This is not untrue. The Hebrew translation includes that context, but it also connects *early* to earnestness and diligence,[6] meaning that if we seek wisdom earnestly and diligently, then we will find it.

I'd like to apply the word *early* to the span of our lives. I believe that it is best to seek wisdom at a young or early age, in the dawn of our lives. If we wait until we are old to try to get wisdom, we will make a lot of mistakes along the way that could have been avoided. We should start young getting instruction and correction, listening to good advice, and obeying the commandments of our mothers and fathers. As we grow, we should seek to make wise decisions. We don't want to live our lives in misery, but we will if we don't seek wisdom early. Some of us who received wisdom late in life can testify to this.

Many people are miserable. They don't want to live. Their lives are a mess. They don't know what to do.

If this is you, then let me tell you that wisdom can change your life. No matter what your life is like, what kind of problems you are facing—marital, family, financial, ministry, or moral—wisdom can turn the tide. There are always solutions with wisdom. Wisdom brings solutions to problem. Love wisdom, and wisdom will love you back by helping you back to the good life God intended for you.

Wisdom brings riches, honor, and righteousness that lasts forever

> Riches and honor are with me, yes, enduring riches and righteousness.
> —Proverbs 8:18

We see all of these traits mentioned in Psalm 112— riches, honor, and righteousness. Verse 3 says, "Wealth and riches shall be in his house, and his righteousness endures forever." We talked about this in chapter 4. Proverbs 8:18 gives us the reason this was true for the Psalm 112 man. It was because he had wisdom.

Wisdom brings riches and honor that endure and last, not money that just comes through your hand and leaves. How many people do you know of who have come into large sums of money only to be broke soon after? That is not wisdom. Wisdom would have led them to invest or employ a strategy to make it last.

When God says He gives you power to get wealth, it's not some magical way of getting wealth. He gives you the power to get wealth because He gives you His wisdom, His Word, His commandments, His statutes, and His judgments. If you follow them, you can expect to prosper.

Wisdom gives you something better than gold and silver

> My fruit is better than gold, yes, than fine gold, and my revenue than choice silver.
>   —PROVERBS 8:19

This verse seems to contradict the one before it. But when you have knowledge, understanding, level-headedness, discretion, prudence, sound judgment, and responsible decision-making skills—the fruit of wisdom—obtaining riches and honor will be no problem for you. God will promote you. He will trust you with more. He will bring you before great men. Having wisdom and its fruit is better than fine gold and choice silver.

Wisdom leads you on the right path

> I lead in the way of righteousness, in the
> midst of the paths of justice.
>
> —PROVERBS 8:20

It is important that you are on the right path.
Wisdom puts you on the right path. It is like the "word
behind you, saying, 'This is the way, walk in it,' when-
ever you turn to the right hand and when you turn to
the left" (Isa. 30:21).

What path are you on? Foolishness and stupidity
will put you on a path of destruction. Wisdom will put
you on a path of life, success, and prosperity. Let it lead
you in the way everlasting (Ps. 139:24, KJV).

Wisdom fills your treasuries

> That I may cause those who love me to inherit
> wealth, and I will fill their treasuries.
>
> —PROVERBS 8:21

Do you love wisdom or do you love foolishness? There
are people who don't love or pursue wisdom. They love
foolishness, gossip, stupidity, ignorance, rebellion, dis-
obedience, and sin. They don't fear the Lord, and the
fear of the Lord is the beginning of wisdom (Prov. 9:10).

Wisdom will help you get substance or wealth. It will fill your storehouse, which for most of us is our bank accounts, pantries, garages, or other storage facilities or depositories. Wisdom will open the windows of heaven over our lives, and we will not have room to receive all that God has for us.

ARE YOU WALKING IN THE WISDOM OF GOD?

One of the problems with our society is that there are too many people who lack wisdom and engage in foolishness. They speak foolishly. They make foolish decisions. They get involved in foolish relationships, and they expect to prosper. When things don't work out in their lives, they blame God. They say things like, "God, why did You let this happen to me?" It's not God's fault; it's the decisions they made. If they make unwise decisions, hang around with foolish people, and have no fear of the Lord, they will have problems in life. They will not be happy.

Proverbs 3:13 says, "Happy is the man who finds wisdom, and the man who gets understanding." You cannot make foolish decisions and prosper. You will not enjoy life. You will get yourself into all kinds of messed-up situations—addiction, abuse, sin, and misuse of money and resources. You don't want to be in a place where you begin to develop bitterness, especially with God. You may find yourself asking, "If God is such a good God, why did He allow this to happen to me?" God allowed it because you allowed it. Your decisions open the door to success, prosperity, happiness, and fulfillment or to failure, poverty, misery, and emptiness. You cannot make foolish decisions, live a foolish life-style, and have foolish people influencing you and still expect to prosper.

"There is a way that seems right to a man, but its end is the way of death" (Prov. 14:12; 16:25). Foolishness will have you confused. You will think you are going right when you are headed for destruction. This is the way of the double-minded, always wavering, never sure. Double-minded people have very low discernment. They are unable to make consistently wise and righteous decisions because of insecurity caused by rejection and pride from rebellion. They are afraid to make decisions and too prideful to ask for or accept wise counsel. When things don't go well in life, they get bitter and blame God and others for their hardships. The double-minded are ruled by foolishness instead of wisdom.

The Book of Proverbs talks a lot about fools: "fools despise wisdom and instruction" (Prov. 1:7); his way is "right in his own eyes" (Prov. 12:15); a fool takes "no delight in understanding, but in expressing his own heart"; a fool's behavior is contemptible and brings dishonor and reproach (Prov. 18:2–3). Fools do not walk in God's wisdom. They are simple and do not make wise decisions. They don't practice prudence, restraint, or caution. Delayed gratification is not in their vocabulary. They don't study, prepare, plan, or save. These choices, mind-sets, and behaviors lead down a path of death and not life.

So, check your life. God is saying, "Today I have set before you life and prosperity, and death and disaster, blessing and curse. I am commanding you to love Me, walk in My ways, and obey My commands, so that you will live a prosperous and fruitful life. I am commanding you—choose life." (See Deuteronomy 30:15–19.) God has laid it out for you. If you are not prospering, ask yourself, "Am I walking in the wisdom of God?"

HOW I CAME TO KNOW THE WISDOM OF GOD

There was a time in my life when I did not know God's wisdom. I didn't know what it meant to "conduct my affairs with discretion." Like many of us over the last few generations, I come from a home where there was no father figure. I was primarily raised by my mother and aunt. During that time, I was not taught the Word of God. My family was not a Christian family. We belonged to a church, but really our names were just on the membership roster. I did not have anyone to teach me what the Word of God said about the way I should live. Much of what I learned I had to learn on my own.

My redemption came at the age of twenty when the pastor of the church I joined became my spiritual father. He taught me and helped me in my walk with God. He taught me how to study the Word and to seek wisdom.

At the age of twenty-one, I got married. My wife and I have been married for more than thirty years. But none of what I saw coming up prepared me to be a good father and faithful partner in marriage. I never saw this growing up. I didn't know of too many families where there was a husband and a wife living together. What I knew about was people who shacked up. I knew about single mothers who had children out of wedlock. I knew about men who had children with different women. I knew about women who had children with different men. Those were the models I saw growing up.

Because of salvation and a spiritual father who taught me the Word of God, I learned the importance of committing to live the principles of wisdom in the Bible. I learned how to be a faithful husband and father. I often tell people that even if you do not have a good role model, you can make a decision in your life to do what is right according to the Word of God.

I was headed down a path of misery, but because of wisdom, my whole life turned around. Sometimes things may not be perfect in life, but because of the grace of God, you do not have to remain foolish and double-minded.

We don't always come up living God's best, but we can still make a decision to do something different from what others have done before us. Get wisdom, and let the foolishness end with you. I was blessed to have a spiritual father who taught me wisdom. I am blessed because the grace of God opened my heart to desire His wisdom. I did not want to pass on to my children the same lack of wisdom that I lived with early in life. God orchestrated my life so that I would find wisdom. He will do this for you too.

ASK FOR WISDOM

If any of you lacks wisdom, let him ask of God, who gives to all men liberally and without criticism, and it will be given to him.

—JAMES 1:5

God loves to give wisdom. You can receive a spirit of wisdom. You can receive an impartation of wisdom. The Bible says that Moses laid hands on Joshua, and Joshua was filled with the spirit of wisdom (Deut. 34:9). Get around wise people so you can receive an impartation of wisdom. Follow wise leaders, pastors, and other people who know the Word and have the wisdom of God. Find a good life coach, someone who is successful and proven, someone who is not just talking it but living it. Ask God to lead you to wise counselors.

God really loves when you ask for wisdom. When is the last time you asked God for wisdom? When you get the wisdom of God, it will give you creative ideas, witty inventions, and innovation. It will cause you to make the right decision concerning your career and will connect you with the right people. Wisdom will keep you from sabotaging your future and will keep you from poverty.

If you are struggling financially, I am not here to condemn you. That is not what this is about. All of us have struggled with finances. All of us can use financial breakthroughs. But if you are dealing with poverty and wrong mind-sets concerning the blessed life God has set up for you, I want you to know that you can begin to turn that around today if you commit to study and meditate on God's Word. Ask the Lord for direction.

Follow the Spirit of God. Listen to and obey His voice. Fear Him and follow His Word, and you will begin to make wise decisions.

If you have been involved in foolish relationships, sexual impurity, drug addiction, and other things that were not wise, repent. Ask God to forgive you. Turn around and say, "Lord, I am coming to You. I am coming to Your wisdom and to Your Word. I don't want to walk in foolishness. I don't want to walk in stupidity. I want to walk in the blessing of God."

Watch your life turn around. It may not happen overnight, because wisdom, knowledge, and understanding take time to get. But increase your capacity for more and more wisdom, and God will give you more. Get good books and read them. Study the Scriptures. Learn about giving, prayer, the prophetic and apostolic, worship and intercession, faith, and the things of the Spirit of God. Learn about miracles, deliverance, and healing. They are all parts of God's wisdom.

Learn about the truths of God. Become a member of a good church where the Word of God is being preached and you can receive teaching and instruction. Don't go somewhere just because you've always gone there. If there is no teaching and instruction, you need to leave and find a good Word church where the man or woman of God brings forth wisdom. When you listen to wise teaching, your life will begin to turn around. Poverty and lack will break off your life. Your business, finances, career, and life will prosper.

GET WISDOM AND IMPART IT TO THE NEXT GENERATION

As your wisdom matures, be ready to share it with others, especially the youth. Passing on the wisdom of God to the next generation is one of the most important things we can do in the kingdom, and God wants to use you to impart it to them. As you grow in wisdom, you may mentor just a few people who will need your help, instruction, counsel, and direction.

With wisdom being the principal thing and so many people in our society failing, there is a greater need for wisdom than ever before. God wants you to impart it to your sons, daughters, grandchildren, the next generation, and the youth of your church. God wants them to get wisdom at a young age so they make wise decisions and live successful and prosperous lives. Teach them wisdom so they get riches, honor, and substance, and so God will fill their treasuries.

Wisdom says, "If you love me, I will love you. If you seek me early, you will find me. I'll give you riches and honor. I will cause you to inherit substance. I'll fill your bank accounts. I'll give you wealth." Wisdom is always connected to wealth. Psalm 112 believers will have riches and honor because they conduct their affairs with wisdom. They will also see this wisdom and wealth multiply in the lives of their children, both natural and spiritual.

In the opening verses to Proverbs 4, King Solomon wrote about the wisdom he received from his father, King David. Solomon was the wisest and wealthiest man in the Bible. His father taught him the value of wisdom to the point that when God told Solomon he could ask for anything and God would give it to him, Solomon asked for wisdom. Parents, and fathers especially, are responsible for not only bringing children into the world but also for teaching them wisdom so they are able to live their lives accordingly.

What is often absent in many homes is a father who imparts wisdom to his children. Just as David taught Solomon that the fear of the Lord is the beginning of wisdom, all fathers must do the same if they want to see their children prosper. However, that can be hard to do if the father doesn't fear God himself. You cannot impart to people what you don't have in your own life. This is why the Bible says, "Get wisdom!" (Prov. 4:5).

David was a man who feared God. He was a man who loved God. God called him a man after His own heart. David gave Solomon a love for the wisdom of God.

The Bible says, "Train up a child in the way he should go, and when he is old he will not depart from it" (Prov. 22:6). Teach them to have a love for wisdom when they are children. Build a foundation of wisdom in your home. Lead your children to seek wisdom early. Tell them that wisdom is the principal thing. It is the most important thing. Let them know they will not make it in life unless they learn how to make good decisions. Talk to them about the mistakes you made and how you made things right. Don't keep these lessons to yourself. We need to be able to pass wisdom on to the next generation so the blessing of God increases generation after generation.

All the affairs and relationships in our lives must be led by wisdom if we want to see the promise of Psalm 112 be the hallmark of our lives. Wisdom is the first and foundational thing that causes us to live out the blessings, favor, and prosperity of God.

SPECIAL DECLARATIONS FOR FATHERS TO RISE UP AND TEACH WISDOM TO THEIR CHILDREN

Lord, I declare: It is my responsibility as a father to teach my sons and daughters, the next generation, the wisdom of God and the fear of the Lord. I will do what God has called me to do.

The fear of the Lord will be in my life.

Lord, I repent for any way that I have not fulfilled my responsibility as a man. I repent for any way that I have not been faithful to be a man of God. Deliver me.

Lord, as I go to sleep at night, visit me in dreams. Show me where I need to step up my responsibilities as a man to my wife and my children.

FOR THE MAN WHO HAS RUN FROM RESPONSIBILITY IN HIS FAMILY

Lord, I come to You and repent for trying to run away from my responsibilities as a father. I break every curse of illegitimacy, and I bind the works of the devil against my being the man of God my children deserve.

Deliver me, Lord, and set me free.

Lord, send revival into my life. Awaken me to righteousness.

Let me arise and become a father. Let me become a man of responsibility, a man who fears You.

May I humble myself before You, Lord, to learn of Your ways and to serve You faithfully all the days of my life.

PRAYERS FOR THE SPIRIT OF WISDOM

Father, may Your Spirit of wisdom be released over my life in the name of Jesus.

I receive the wisdom of God and the fear of the Lord. Let them be a part of my life.

Lead me and guide me to make wise decisions. Teach me the wisdom of Your Word.

Wisdom is my companion. She will bless me, protect me, exalt me, and promote me.

Wisdom is the principal thing.

I receive wisdom—the wisdom of the Word and the Spirit of wisdom.

Jesus is my wisdom. He is in my life.

I receive the wisdom of heaven to walk on this earth.

Lord, release to me the peace and prosperity that come as a result of being wise.

May Your wisdom increase in my heart that You may do great things in me in the days to come.

Thank You, Lord, for blessing me with wisdom.

PRAYERS AND DECREES FOR YOUNG PEOPLE TO FIND WISDOM

Let young people seek wisdom early.

Let them, like Daniel and Joseph, have wisdom at a young age to interpret dreams and to understand the dream realm.

Let young people have wisdom like Daniel, who had ten times the wisdom of all the astrologers of Babylon.

Let God give them wisdom ten times more than the wisdom of the world.

May God allow them to walk in the wisdom of the prophetic and of prophets.

May God allow them to prosper.

Father, I praise and I thank You for doing great things in their lives.

I decree it. I prophesy it. I speak it in Jesus's name. Amen.

Chapter 7

RIGHTEOUS FOREVER

He will never be shaken; the righteous
will be remembered forever.
—Psalm 112:6, amp

T HE Psalm 112 man is uncompromisingly righteous. His righteousness endures. It lasts. It stands through tests and trials. This man does what is right all the time. There is no wavering. He doesn't do right sometimes, then at other times do wrong. For him, doing right is not a struggle. When it comes to doing right or wrong, he doesn't have to make a decision; he has already decided that he will do right. When wrong things come up, he is not overwhelmed with the temptation, because he has already settled in his heart that he will do right.

The reason people struggle with temptation, can't overcome certain things, and always end up doing something wrong is because they have not settled in their hearts and made a decision that when right and wrong come up, there is no choice. The stable person, on the other hand, already knows he is going to choose to go the right way. He does not have to stand there and try to figure out which way he will go. He has already made the decision that he will stand for what is right and godly.

As a stable-minded believer, if you see something that doesn't belong to you and something says, "Steal it," that is not an option. You have already made a decision that you are not a thief. You do what is right. You have consistent success in this area because you don't wait until the point of temptation to make a choice. You have already decided ahead of time to do what is right. It is settled, and your heart is so established (Ps. 112:8) that all you'll do is right. Like the Psalm 112 man, your righteousness can endure forever (v. 9).

The reason I preach this so strongly is because I see so many who are up and down. They do well for a while, and then they backslide. As believers, we should be looking to live a consistent lifestyle. Our righteousness should go on forever.

Does your righteousness extend beyond a season? Or are you double-minded—one moment you're doing well; the next, something happens and you are thrown off? That is not stability. That is double-mindedness.

Of course we all struggle, but remember that is not the goal—just to get by and remain struggling; being on fire for God one minute and totally giving up and discouraged, living life like the wicked the next. Our goal is to become steadfast, unshakeable, single-minded, and fixed on God.

WHO IS RIGHTEOUS?

I am convinced that most Christians don't understand the characteristics of a righteous person. Some people think a righteous person is someone who does right sometimes but not at other times. They think righteousness is about being "basically good." Then they may compare themselves with someone who is doing worse. This gives them a false sense of goodness, and they put themselves in the "righteous" category. You can always find somebody doing worse than you. If you are fornicating with one person, you can always find a person who is fornicating with two. It's easy to look at someone in full rebellion and say, "Oh well, I'm not that bad."

If we are to learn how to live the Psalm 112 promise, we need to know what the standard is. Who is righteous, and what does that look like? Because so many in the church are bound by double-mindedness, we need to redefine who a godly, righteous person really is. The first thing we need to know is that this person has been redeemed by Christ. She has accepted by faith His sacrifice on the cross and has become a new creation. I'll come back to this. Second, this person has been delivered. She has gone through deliverance and knows how to wage effective spiritual warfare to maintain her position in Christ. You cannot be bound to sin and be righteous.

The Hebrew word for *righteous* is *tsaddiyq*.[1] It means just and lawful in government, in one's cause, in conduct and character, and "as justified and vindicated by God." It also means right and correct. A righteous person is one "who maintains the right and dispenses justice."[2] We discussed justice in the last chapter as it relates to discretion and wisdom. Righteousness also refers to a person "who speaks what is right and true"— honesty.[3] The righteous are just toward others and obedient to the laws of God. They are "upright, honest, virtuous, pious."[4] They are temperate and sober in what they eat and drink, they love the truth and wisdom, and they do good.[5] They do not compromise when it comes to doing the right thing. According to the Hebrew word for *everlasting*, the righteousness of the Psalm 112 believer is perpetual, continuous, indefinite, unending, and eternal. Her righteousness is incorruptible.[6]

The righteous have made a decision to walk with God—no turning back, ever. They have been justified and made right by Christ and now are in good standing with God. Their sins have been covered by the blood of Jesus. They are being perfected and sanctified by the Spirit of God. They walk according the Spirit and godly wisdom. And they will not do anything to compromise this position. They know that sin and unrighteousness separates them from God. Connection to God means everything to them, and no matter what mama, daddy, friends, husband, wife, children, or church folk think, they will remain rooted and grounded in God. Their default is, "You can do what you want to do, but as for me and my house, we will serve the Lord." (See Joshua 24:15.)

Temptation and attacks of the enemy do not shake or overwhelm the righteous. They maintain a level of peace and trust because they believe God when He says, "No weapon formed against you shall prosper" (Isa. 54:17, NKJV). They do not get tempted by simple things because their minds have been set on the things of God. They know that as they think, so shall they be (Prov. 23:7). Their minds are made up about who they are and what they do, and it is all centered around honoring and pleasing God. When the devil comes at them, they say, "Look, I don't know why you are coming to me with that. I made that decision ten years ago, and the answer is still no." This is how a godly, righteous, fixed individual whose heart is established responds to the enemy.

There are too many double-minded, unstable people in the church. Their hearts are not established. Their minds have not been set. They are still struggling with the same issues and problems they struggled with five years ago. Who wants to live a life full of instability? Who wants to be up and down? Who wants to be in and out?

If you really want the blessing of the Lord, delight in the law of the Lord, make a decision to always do things God's way, and live according to His standard. It doesn't make any difference how many others don't want to live this way. If you have to be the only one in the group, determine that you are going to live right and clean. Think about Lot.

Lot, Abraham's nephew and a righteous man, lived in the city of Sodom with his wife and two daughters. The wickedness in the city got so bad that angels showed up to get Lot and his family out. The men in the city wanted to sleep with the angels. When the men knocked the door down, Lot said, "I'll send my daughters out to you." And they said, "We don't want your daughters. We want the men." (See Genesis 19.) That's messed up. And the angels had to blind everybody just to get Lot and his family out of town.

Can you imagine? Could you be uncompromisingly righteous living in Sodom, where everybody is perverted and yours is the only family in the whole city that is righteous? Have you made a decision that you will not go along with the crowd, that just because everybody else is doing something, it doesn't mean it's for you? I have news for you: it only looks like everybody else is getting away with it; nobody is getting away with anything. God has a standard, and He is a righteous judge.

This is why I meditate on Psalm 112 over and over again. I confess to God that this is the kind of man I want to be. I want to be a stable, steadfast, and fixed man whose heart is trusting in God. I want to be an uncompromisingly righteous man. I want to be a blessed man. I want to have wealth and riches in my house.

A SHADOW OF
THE ONE NEW MAN

The promise of Psalm 112 is real and true. We can see that from the Old Testament to the New Testament this man's righteousness remained and was remembered even at the time of the early church. Look at 2 Corinthians 9:9: "He [the benevolent and generous person] scattered abroad, he gave to the poor, his righteousness endures forever!" (AMP). Paul was talking about the Psalm 112 man. This verse refers back to Psalm 112:9: "He has given away freely; he has given to the poor; his righteousness endures forever; his horn shall be exalted with honor." Though we will discuss the righteous man and his giving in chapter 9, I want to point out the significance of his being mentioned in Paul's letter to the Corinthians, which returns me to the point about the righteous person becoming a new creation in Christ.

As I studied how the apostles interpreted Old Covenant scriptures and applied them to the New Testament church, I began to see that this man who is spoken of in Psalm 112 is a prophetic picture or foreshadow of the new man ("If any man be in Christ, he is a new creature" [2 Cor. 5:17, KJV]). We are one new man. (See Ephesians 2:14–16.) When you become born again, you become a new person. You become a new creature. You become a righteous person. You accept the righteousness of God that is in Christ.

So even though it is in Psalm 112, during the Old Covenant, it is a prophetic picture of the church. The church in Corinth was told to give based on a word in Psalm 112. All of the prophetic words from the Old Testament were fulfilled with the coming of Christ. Everything in the Old Testament was a prophetic picture of something new God was going to do: new creature, new creation, new man. His one new man is the coming together of Jew and Gentile. This new thing that God was about to do was prophesied in the Old Covenant. We are the result of the prophetic utterance spoken thousands of years ago, which was fulfilled in Christ. As I have already pointed out, as the righteousness of Christ, we can rightly claim the blessings of Psalm 112. We are the Psalm 112 man.

HAVE YOU CONSIDERED JOB?

Job is another picture of the Psalm 112 man. Most people know only that Satan attacked Job and that he lost everything. They know he was a righteous man. The Bible calls him a perfect man, "upright, and one that feared God, and eschewed evil" (Job 1:1, KJV). There was nobody like him in all the earth. He was the most outstanding example of a righteous man in his generation. But what made him righteous? It wasn't his keeping some laws, rules, regulations, or some "religious stuff." See, religious stuff doesn't make you righteous. It's not because he was under the Law.

Job is the oldest book in the Bible. Some scholars believe that Job predated Abraham, so he didn't have the Ten Commandments to guide him. He was not counted righteous because he followed the Law of Moses or because he brought every sacrifice and dotted every *i* and crossed every *t*. He wouldn't have known to do that.

We are not talking about legalism here. We're not talking about trying to do everything perfectly and judging everybody like the Pharisees in Jesus's day did. They had a book of rules and regulations that listed a certain distance you could walk on the Sabbath. Some of our more traditional churches used to be like this back in the day: you don't go to the show, don't put on makeup, and don't watch TV more than twenty-one minutes a day. You could go crazy trying to keep a rule book. Since Job didn't have one, we know that how well he kept the Law was not what God used to determine Job's righteousness.

Chapter 29 of Job carries the secret to Job's righteousness. It is one of my favorite chapters in the Book of Job because it gives a picture of Job before he was attacked by the enemy—the picture of a righteous man.

Job served God from his youth (v. 4)

If you want to be blessed, start out serving God when you are young. We discovered something similar about wisdom. Wisdom and righteousness are connected. Don't wait until you're ninety-five when you see

139

the death angel down the block. Serve God while you are young.

Job was prosperous (v. 6)

I confess Job 29:6 as one of my prosperity confessions: "Let my steps be bathed with butter. Let the rock pour me out rivers of oil." Butter represents prosperity. Oil represents the anointing. Job was anointed to prosper.

Job was influential (vv. 7–10)

When Job showed up, everybody shut up. He had respect. He was a powerful man. He was a righteous man. God had exalted him.

Job cared for people who had no one to help them (vv. 12–13)

Job didn't just talk the talk; he walked the walk. He delivered the poor and fatherless. He was the wealthiest man alive (Job 1:3), but he was compassionate. He didn't think he was better than the poor. He never walked by them and said, "Look at them." He also looked out for widows.

Many people claim to be righteous, but what are they doing? Do they have any works? They speak in tongues? That's fine. They shout? That's fine too. But what about giving to the poor, widows, and fatherless? What about going in your pocket and helping people who can't help themselves? Do these so-called righteous people do any of that? Or do they walk by people and say, "Look at them"? Do they mock people and put them down? That is not righteousness.

A righteous person is gracious and full of compassion. A righteous person has mercy. A righteous person understands that God gave them everything they have. It's the blessing of God upon their life. They do not dare look at other people who are made in the image of God and mistreat, abuse, and oppress them. I cannot say I love God, whom I don't see, if I can't love my brother whom I do see.

Job was a father to the poor (v. 16)

Poor people need fathers. There is so much poverty in inner cities because there are few fathers. I thank God for what mothers have done. They have done a great job. But we need men to rise up and be fathers. We need men who will stand up and be fathers to the poor, who will not only take care of their own but take care of somebody else's too. I don't know where I would be if it were not for my spiritual father, who saw value in me some forty years ago. I was poor not only financially but also in spirit, wisdom, knowledge, and understanding. Righteous men father those who need a godly example.

Job is the same type of individual Psalm 112 talks about. He poured out the wisdom God gave him to both his natural and spiritual seed, and God increased them all.

There is a thread here of the righteous person, the Psalm 112 believer. It is not enough for him to get the blessings of God; he must also pass them on. He must spread the wealth of God's kingdom blessings to everyone who is in need spiritually, emotionally, and financially. His compassion for the weak and afflicted drives him to spread his wealth. This is how he fulfills the commandments of God, which boils down to "you shall love the Lord your God with all your heart, and with all your soul, and with all your mind.... You shall love your neighbor as yourself" (Matt. 22:37–39).

Job was an uncompromisingly righteous man. No wonder God bragged on him and asked, "Have you considered My servant Job" (Job 1:8). He helped the poor, fatherless, and widows. He brought deliverance. He was compassionate. He was godly from his youth. And so God bragged on him and said, "There's none like him in all the land." The devil thought that if God took the hedge from around him, Job would curse Him. But Job, being fixed and established in God, never cursed God, not one time. Even when his wife started talking crazy, saying, "Curse God and die" (Job 2:9), he remained righteous in the eyes of God. He knew the God he served.

You may not always understand what is happening, but don't ever turn your back on God. If you remain steadfast, when it is all over, God may bless you with twice as much as you had before, just as He did with Job (Job 42:12). God is a God of restoration.

HAS GOD CONSIDERED YOU?

The idea that God bragged on Job and could potentially brag on any one of us can be scary. If God said, "Devil, have you considered my servant John or Sue or Mary?" some of us would say, "No, no—hold it, Lord. I'm not really all that good."

Although we may not want to face the kind of attack that came upon Job, we do want to have the favor and approval of God. And so, when I read Psalm 112, I compare myself to that. Then I wonder if God can say the things He said about Job about me—that there is nobody like me. Do I stand out in the crowd?

Some people want to be a part of the crowd. I don't know about you, but I don't want to be like everyone else. I don't want to be ordinary. I don't want to be normal. I want to be above average in God. I want God to point at me and say, "Now there's somebody right there. There's a just and righteous man."

God has always put His finger on certain people. In the Bible, we see God's hand on people such as Daniel, Joseph, Job, and individuals who were faithful and righteous. God always pointed them out. He marked David as a man after His own heart (Acts 13:22).

I want God to be able to mark me as a righteous man. I don't want to make my standard the standard of my generation. Our standards have gone down so much. I want to stand out in my generation as a righteous man, one who fears and trusts in God, one whose heart is fixed. I want to give. I want to disburse to the poor. I want to help. I want to bless others.

I can hear the limiting thinking of the religious people: "There is none who is righteous. No, not one. All of us are worms. Everybody is messed up." When I say "perfect" or "righteous," I'm not saying that you don't make a mistake. Perfect means whole. It means developed and mature.

God wants to bring us to a level where we walk in love, we are not stingy or selfish, we are not putting everything in our pockets, and we are not neglecting those who are hurting. From our godly and righteous place, we look out for people. We look out for one another. We take care of one another. We're compassionate. We're gracious. We're merciful. We're righteous. We're givers. We trust in God. Our hearts are fixed. We're not moved. We know God's standard, and we keep it. We're not shaken by what comes or goes. We don't change with the season. We don't change with the tide. We're not double-minded. We're not unstable. We're steadfast. We have made a decision to walk according to the law of God. We are going to do what God says to do. We know we are new creatures in Christ. We are determined to remain uncompromisingly righteous.

A HIGHER STANDARD

Never let what people say stop you from doing what is right. Never let a wicked person stop you from being the righteous person you are supposed to be. Never let them discourage you or frustrate you. Keep your eyes on the Lord. Determine that you will not be moved by wicked, jealous, petty, selfish, stingy, perverse, and ungodly people who mock righteousness. Remain merciful and forgiving, but know that you're above all that garbage. You live above it, not in it or below it. You have a higher standard. You have the Word of God. You have the love of God. Don't let people pull you down to their standards. Let them know you live a clean life, that you believe in holiness, and that you don't speak like everybody else, cussing and using profanity. You have a higher standard. You don't talk about people. You don't live a raggedy, ungodly lifestyle. You don't get drunk. You are not perverse. You have a higher standard. Don't compromise it.

Uncompromisingly righteous is who you are. It flows from within, from the Holy Spirit. You may wonder, "Why can't I be like everybody else? How do they get away with it?" You know how it is for you: if you say something wrong, you get convicted. If you hurt somebody's feelings, you say, "Please forgive me." Some people can run over others, back up over them, and not feel a thing. Not you. You have a higher standard.

You are saved. You love God. Don't ever apologize for that. You can't do what everybody else does. Sometimes you may cry about it. You may feel alone, asking, "Why can't I be a dog? Why can't I run with the pack?" God didn't call you to be a pack animal. He called you to be an eagle. You fly high all by yourself. You mount up with wings as eagles. You are not a dog or a chicken. You don't hang out with packs. God called Abraham out from among his family and told him to leave all by himself. I'd rather be blessed alone than cursed with a group.

There is a cost in this world to being uncompromisingly righteous, but God wants you to know there are more like you. You are not alone. There is a remnant of believers who want to love God and live according to His standards just as badly as you do. But whether you meet them or not, know that you are called to stand and remain righteous forever. He is with you. He is able to make all grace abound toward you, that you always have all sufficiency in all things.

DECLARATIONS TO REMAIN UNCOMPROMISINGLY RIGHTEOUS

I cast out the pack spirit. I will not run with the crowd. I will be bold and have the courage to stand up. When I say no to sin and unrighteousness, I mean no.

I call forth boldness to stand up against the wicked, messed-up people who mock the righteousness of God in me. They can all leave God if they want to. I love them, but even they will not cause me to fall out of position with God.

I am uncompromisingly righteous. I will not compromise. I will be a giver. I will be compassionate and full of mercy and grace.

Thank You, Lord, for making me a new creature.

Thank You, Lord, that the standard I have is higher than the normal.

I am not afraid. My heart is fixed. I will not be double-minded. I will not waver. I will be steadfast and unmovable, always abounding in the work of the Lord.

Thank You, Lord, for blessing me and exalting my horn with honor.

Thank You, Lord, for saving and protecting me.

I set myself on a course of righteousness. I will live according to Your standards all the days of my life.

Forgive me, Lord, if I've ever wavered, doubted, or compromised.

I want to be stable. I want to be steadfast. I want to be consistent and faithful.

Thank You, Lord. I will be a Psalm 112 believer all the days of my life.

Chapter 8

FIXED AND ESTABLISHED

He shall not be afraid of evil tidings; his heart is fixed, trusting in the LORD. His heart is established; he shall not be afraid, until he sees triumph upon his enemies.
—PSALM 112:7–8

ONE OF THE main characteristics of the double-minded rejection personality is fear. Psalm 112 believers are not fearful people. They are not afraid of bad news and evil tidings. They have great expectations about their lives because they have put their trust in the Lord.

We cannot prosper if there is fear in our lives. Fear immobilizes us and keeps us from living in freedom and peace. Fear takes on many forms. The most common types of fear among believers include the following:

- Fear of rejection
- Fear of authority
- Fear of people

- Fear of being hurt
- Fear of confrontation
- Fear of Jezebel
- Fear of God
- Fear of failure
- Fear of losing your salvation
- Fear of going to hell
- Fear of demons
- Fear of witchcraft
- Fear of being alone
- Fear of getting married
- Fear of being robbed
- Fear of going broke
- Fear of not getting married
- Fear of not having enough
- Fear of not joining a church
- Fear of joining a church
- Fear of leaving a church

- Fear of the pastor
- Fear of leadership

Fears and phobias are all a part of the rejection personality. God does not want us to be fearful people. When you are fearful, you withdraw, hide, and run because you don't want to be hurt or taken advantage of. Like a turtle, you go into a shell. Like an ostrich, you stick your head in the sand. You put up a shield and a defense. You don't want anyone to get close. You don't open up. You build up walls. You isolate yourself because you can't trust anyone.

That is not prosperity. Prosperity is having good relationships, not being a loner and being isolated. The Bible says Psalm 112 believers are not afraid because their hearts are fixed, trusting in the Lord. They are not doubting, wavering, or struggling with unbelief. They trust God. Their hearts are fixed on God.

This is the key to being stable-minded. If you go back to James 1:5–7, it says, "If any of you lacks wisdom, let him ask of God, who gives to all men liberally and without criticism, and it will be given to him. But let him ask in faith, without wavering. For he who wavers is like a wave of the sea, driven and tossed with the wind. Let not that man think that he will receive anything from the Lord." In other words, a wavering, double-minded person is a person who trusts God sometimes and other times doubts, because his heart is not fixed. This goes back to being a heart issue.

The Psalm 112 believer's heart is established. These individuals trust in God, knowing He is their protector and deliverer. Psalm 112 believers don't have to worry about anything coming against them. They know that if God is for them, who can be against them? (See Romans 8:31.) These believers are stabilized and confident not in themselves but in God. This is how we should all want to live. We should not be tossed to and fro upon the waves of life.

A heart that is established is set, and as I said before, the decision to do the right thing has already been made in advance and cannot be changed or altered. The word *establish* brings to mind the foundation of a house, how it is set deep into the earth. When the winds and floods come, the house doesn't move or shake, because it has been established.

You cannot have a prosperous walk with God without being established and set. When you go in to get your physical heart checked, the technicians and doctors are looking for a consistent heartbeat. Any irregularities are cause for concern. It could mean that you need any number of emergency medical interventions.

God is looking for the same thing: a consistent heart-beat for Him—joyful, peaceful, stable; righteous, holy, stable; kind, stable; compassionate, stable; merciful, stable; faithful, loyal, stable; loving, stable; consistent in your giving, worship, attendance, fellowship…month after month; year after year.

Can you say that about yourself? If not, you need deliverance. Healing and deliverance from the Lord can bring stability to your life. You cannot prosper without addressing this area of your life. Stability, steadfastness, and single-mindedness are the core and foundation of a prosperous believer's life. You cannot build anything else that will last without shoring up this area. The Bible says that a double-minded person is unstable in all his ways. This means he will not prosper long-term in anything without first becoming stable and fixed in his heart.

STAYING POWER

Double-minded people are easily moved. Things easily shake them. They are easily discouraged and depressed. When something comes up against them, they have a difficult time handling it. Many times their only recourse is to shut down and withdraw from everything and everybody, sometimes for weeks at a time. This is not to say that there aren't times when God leads you to come away from everything to pray and seek Him. But for double-minded people, it is more than this. They become shaken and messed up by the difficulties of life to the point that they cannot stand. They get wiped out. They stop attending church and receiving or answering the calls and visits of concerned friends and family. They get overtaken. These are the same people who just last week or last month were decreeing and declaring the Word, shouting, worshipping, and on fire for God. What happened? They don't have what used to be called "staying power." Something hits them, and they get moved—depressed, discouraged—and temporarily give up.

We all deal with life, but this behavior is not part of the personality of the Psalm 112 believer—the stable man. The Bible says that he shall not be moved—forever! What a powerful statement. This man is unmovable, unshakeable.

Now, understand that this is not about being so powerful that nothing fazes you. There are no super saints. But sometimes when you are being moved, shaken, or filled with doubt, you may find yourself asking questions like the following:

- Does God love me?

- Am I really saved?

- Am I going to make it?

- Does the Word really work?

- Did I really hear from God?

- Am I in the right church?

If you find yourself asking questions like these, then you have been shaken, and that is not good. It is not godly. It is not the characteristic of a Psalm 112 believer. The Bible says, "Be steadfast, unmovable, always abounding in the work of the Lord" (1 Cor. 15:58). Be consistent. Be unwavering.

Now I too have experienced heavy discouragement at various points in my thirty-plus years as a believer. At times, I didn't want to get out of the bed. I slept all day and did not look forward to the next. What believer hasn't gone through that? We may feel that this isn't as bad or as sinful as what some others may do. We think, "Well, I'm not smoking, drinking, lying, cussing, fornicating…" Still, think about it: being completely knocked down by something in life is not the mark of a stable individual. That is a double-minded reaction to something that happens to you, something someone says to you or about you.

The danger of this is being stuck in a life God does not want for you. As we have already discovered, God wants you to be happy, successful, and prosperous. Your abundant life is proof that His covenant is true. When you live in a state of wavering and insecurity, you give place for the enemy to come and take up residence in your life. The by-product of being fixed and established is victory over demons such as foolishness, destruction, procrastination, and confusion. As I pointed out in an earlier chapter, these are destiny and prosperity thieves.

BEWARE OF SELF-TRUST

Double-mindedness breeds unbelief, insecurity, faith-lessness, worry, doubt, and fear—mostly fear that God won't come through, that He isn't trustworthy, and that His ways will keep us from happiness and good-ness. The lies that shape the double-minded personal-ity are deadly to our spiritual lives. Double-mindedness is a stronghold and an imagination that exalts itself against the knowledge of God (2 Cor. 10:4–5)—His character and His ways.

This is why we look to the Psalm 112 man. He knows his God is the Lord. He has overcome the lies of double-mindedness. He knows God's heart and mind toward him, that His intentions and plans for him are good (Jer. 29:11). He does not doubt and waver in this.

But some of us struggle when trouble comes. We feel anxious, and that in order for us to see something happen in our lives, we have to make it happen. We take matters out of God's hands and put them in our own, as if to say we trust ourselves more than we trust God. How can that be true?

Our culture encourages us to be self-confident and believe in ourselves. It is virtually impossible to strike a balance between self-trust and trusting in the Lord. As a matter of fact, I don't think there is a balance to be achieved at all. All of our trust must be placed in the Lord. He must take the highest and most supreme place in our lives if we are to see His power work.

If we have any confidence, it should be because we know the power of God that works in us (Eph. 3:20). We can trust His Word when it says, "For God is the One working in you, both to will and to do His good pleasure" (Phil. 2:13). "In Him we live and move and have our being" (Acts 17:28). Anything that we believe or act on outside of this sets us up for failure and disappointment. Where are the people who say, "Some trust in chariots and horses [man's way of doing things], but I will trust in the name of the Lord"? (See Psalm 20:7.)

When we doubt and begin to worry about the future, about whether the house or car note will be paid, whether we'll get the job, or if our children will be saved, we should be immediately aware that we have gotten into the place of finding solutions without seeking God. When we try to manipulate and control the outcomes and results of the things we hope for, we are saying that we are the only ones we can really trust. This is where fear and the need to be in control begin to push us into pride. Pride in ourselves, though bred in insecurity, can lead to self-worship and idolatry.

Double-mindedness lies to us. We are not able to handle the things meant for God to handle. When things don't work out, we respond with bitterness, anger, and rebellion. We get mad at God and don't want to obey Him, all because of what we did to sabotage the success that could have been ours.

We are not the foundation upon which we should be building our faith. When we fail, we have nothing to lean on. The stable man places his trust in God, and thereby he has full and complete victory. He triumphs over his enemies.

I don't think we realize how quickly and easily we look to ourselves and other things to pull us through the challenges we face in life. The sooner we ask the Lord to search us and show us the areas in our hearts that are not fixed and established in Him, the sooner we can get on with living the life He designed.

STOP WAVERING AND TRUST GOD

> How long will you waver between two opinions? If the LORD is God, follow him; but if Baal is God, follow him.
>
> —1 KINGS 18:21, NIV

In chapter 1, I wrote about unbelief and instability manifesting as backsliding. Backsliding is generally about going back and forth between two ruling thoughts—God's and our own, God's and the world's, God's and the enemy's, God's and any other's that is not God. When we choose to listen to and follow another way other than God's, we are guilty of backsliding. This action is also related to apostasy or spiritual adultery. Adultery is unfaithfulness to covenant. These are signs of double-mindedness.

The Hebrew words for *backsliding* are *meshubah*, meaning "apostasy: backsliding, turning away,"[1] and *sarar*, meaning "to turn away, i.e. (morally) be refractory—away, backsliding, rebellious, revolter(-ing), slide back, stubborn, withdrew."[2] Other words from the Hebrew, *shobab* and *shobeb*, render the English meanings "apostate, i.e. idolatrous—backsliding, frowardly, turn away (from margin);" "heathenish or (actually) heathen—backsliding."[3]

Israel was a double-minded nation, going in and out of covenant with God. They were not consistent in their loyalty to God. Israel was guilty of revolt, rebellion, turning away, stubbornness, idolatry, and acting like the heathen nations they were surrounded by.

The stable believer maintains firm hold on the voice of God and seeks only His wisdom. Again, he trusts in the Lord and does not waver.

Take a look at Psalm 26:1: "Judge me, O Lord, for I have walked in my integrity. I have trusted in the Lord; I will not slip." It's "...I shall not slide" in the King James Version. The New International Version says, "...and have not faltered." And the New Living Translation says, "...without wavering." The Hebrew word used in this verse for "slide," "slip," or "waver" is *maad*, also meaning "make to shake."[4]

Shortly after the coming of the Holy Spirit on the Day of Pentecost, many believers were strengthened and held fast to the apostles' doctrine, fellowship, breaking of bread, and prayers. (See Acts 2:42.) This is the opposite of being double-minded.

As the believers grew in number and in faith, persecution grew and caused discouragement. They were warned against falling from steadfastness: "You therefore, beloved, since you know these things beforehand, beware lest you also fall from your own firm footing, being led away by the deception of the wicked" (2 Pet. 3:17).

Strong's defines *steadfastness* using the Greek words *stereóma* and *stérigmos*, both meaning "something established, i.e. (abstractly) confirmation (stability)—steadfastness;" "stability (figuratively)—steadfastness."[5]

By the time the letter of James was written, there was great suffering among the early Christians, and there were many whose faithfulness was waning. Many were departing from the faith and being double-minded in their walk with God. Apostasy was a major problem in the early church, and this was the result of double-mindedness. James encouraged them to remain steadfast in the New Covenant and their commitment to Christ.

As an example, the Colossian church was commended for their steadfastness:

> For though I am absent in the flesh, yet I am with you in spirit, rejoicing and seeing your orderliness and the steadfastness of your faith in Christ.
>
> —COLOSSIANS 2:5

We are living in a time when backsliding and apostasy are rampant among believers. Great moral failures are leading to church hurt and church splits. Divisive false doctrines and controlling religious spirits are causing people to lose trust in the church Jesus established. But I want to encourage you that as you become more and more like the man in Psalm 112, you will be able to stand. You will remain fixed and rooted. Your hope and trust are not in man. You trust in the Lord. Jeremiah 17:7–8 says:

> Blessed is the man who trusts in the LORD, and whose hope is the LORD. For he shall be as a tree planted by the waters, and that spreads out its roots by the river, and shall not fear when heat comes, but its leaf shall be green, and it shall not be anxious in the year of drought, neither shall cease from yielding fruit.

The heat is on, but you are planted, unmovable, fixed, established, and secure. You flourish and yield fruit even in the year of drought. You will not be moved.

LIVE BY FAITH

Faith is a weapon against doubt and fear. It is a stabilizer. Faith in God is one of the main themes in the Bible. It is the foundation for being able to walk in the ways of God. It is the foundation for our salvation: "For by grace you have been saved through faith, and this is not of yourselves. It is the gift of God, not of works, so that no one should boast" (Eph. 2:8–9). We are encouraged to build faith: "Beloved, build yourselves up in your most holy faith" (Jude 20). We build faith by hearing and hearing by the Word of God (Rom. 10:17). Having faith pleases God and brings rewards and blessing into our lives (2 Thess. 1:3). As people in pursuit of the Psalm 112 promise, faith is the basis by which we are to live (Hab. 2:4; Gal. 3:11; Heb. 10:38).

The Greek word for *faith* is *pistis*, meaning faith, belief, trust, confidence; fidelity, faithfulness.[6] A Hebrew word for faith is *amanah*, meaning agreement, firm regulation. In other words, it is agreeing with God and His Word, saying amen. *Amen* means "to lean on for support."[7] It is also translated as "believe." It is used in relation to the faith needed to receive salvation and gives the picture of someone leaning on God (Gen. 15:6).

Another Hebrew word related to faith is *yaqal* (Job

13:15), which means "to trust in extreme pain; to trust under pressure."[8] It is usually translated "hope." Then there is *qawah*, the strongest Hebrew word for *faith*. It is translated as "wait."[9] This word gives a clear picture of why us getting ahead of God shows a lack of faith. We aren't patient. We get anxious, thinking He hasn't heard our cry. Waiting on God communicates faith in His timing. When we have faith, we express to God our confidence in His love for us and that we trust Him to work things out in His timing—and He is always on time.

Unbelief and doubt will hinder a person from receiving the promises of God. Fear is an enemy of faith and will hinder one from receiving. If we have mountains to move in our lives, and if there are things we hope for and expect, it takes faith to see them move:

> Truly I say to you, if you have faith and do not doubt…if you say to this mountain, "Be removed, and be thrown into the sea," it will be done. And whatever you ask in prayer, if you believe, you will receive.
> —MATTHEW 21:21–22

GOD IS IN CONTROL

Trust in the LORD, and do good.
                    —PSALM 37:3

Trust that God has everything under control; just obey and do good. Don't allow yourself to get caught up in trying to make things happen. Don't get caught up in solving problems according to the ways of the world. Remain faithful, righteous, and steadfast. He will take care of the rest: "Commit your way to the LORD; trust in Him also and He will do it" (Ps. 37:5, AMP).

> Rest in the LORD, and wait patiently for Him; do not fret because of those who prosper in their way…Better is a little that the righteous has than the abundance of many wicked.
> —PSALM 37:7, 16

Rest in the Lord. Relax. Take it easy. Stop being so nervous. Don't make minor stuff major. Rest and wait patiently, because God is going to do something. Do not worry and get anxious. Sometimes we get discouraged when we see what seems to be breakthrough and prosperity all around us. Sometimes it seems like we don't have all we need, but we need to trust in the God of more than enough. God can bless a little.

In the miracle of the five loaves and two fish (John 6), God did more with a few loaves of bread and couple of fish than any of us would have imagined. His blessing on that little bit of food increased it, and it became enough to feed five thousand people.

When you get a little, bless it. It's going to go further than if you had more. As I said before, with blessing comes increase.

God is not limited by how small something is. Start blessing what you have in your hands. Don't try to figure out how it's going to work. You can have a lot of money, and it can leave your hands too if you're not living right. This is why wisdom can boast that its fruit is better than fine gold and choice silver. Some people get stuck on the treasure and not the One who gives and takes away, who blesses and curses. When you walk in the favor and blessing of the Lord, you don't ever need to worry about money. You will always have more than enough. You just trust God. Do good. Follow His wisdom. The promise of Psalm 112 is yours.

DECLARATIONS OF UNWAVERING TRUST

I am unshakeable. I will not be moved.

My heart is fixed, trusting in the Lord.

My heart is established; I will not be afraid.

Because I trust in the Lord, I will see triumph over my enemies.

Because I trust in the Lord, I do not fear evil tidings.

I trust in the Lord and remain faithful to the path He has placed me on.

I trust in the Lord and do good. I will dwell in the land and practice faithfulness.

Because I commit my way to the Lord, because I trust in Him, He will bring His promises to pass in my life.

I rest in the Lord and wait patiently for Him.

I serve the God of more than enough; therefore, God will bless what little I have in my hand.

I will not be shaken by heat, drought, or famine. I will flourish and be satisfied. I will not be ashamed.

I delight myself in the abundance of peace.

Chapter 9

GENEROUS

*He has given away freely; he has given to
the poor; his righteousness endures forever;
his horn shall be exalted with honor.*
—Psalm 112:9

ONE OF THE leading characteristics of stable and secure people is their generosity. Stable believers are consistent givers. It is a part of their righteous character, something that has already been established in their hearts. They consistently support the work of God and consistently help the poor, fatherless, and widows. My encouragement to you as a believer seeking the promises in Psalm 112 is to never get out of the habit of giving; it is the characteristic of a righteous person. It is also an act of worship.

It is God's desire for you to be consistent in your giving. Your generosity pleases Him. The Bible says because they give to the poor, they lack nothing (Prov. 28:27); he who lends to the poor, the Lord will repay him (Prov. 19:17); and God loves a cheerful giver. He loves to repay those who are generous. You are blessed immeasurably when you give. Luke 6:38 says that when you give, "good measure, pressed down, shaken together, and running over will be put into your bosom" (NKJV).

Giving is an enjoyable practice for the righteous. It flows out of the way they conduct their affairs with wisdom and discretion. Giving that is coerced, emotional, or decided at a moment's notice is not the kind of giving that flows from a cheerful, grateful, and fixed heart. This is the picture of the generous: they are happy to give and come to the aid of those in need.

Because giving is a big part of receiving the favor and blessing of God, the enemy can make it hard for a believer to give. There are times when believers are faced with seasons of financial difficulty. They may lose their jobs. They may come up against some other kind of financial roadblock. These are times when giving is challenging, and perhaps they may give less than they customarily do.

Another way the enemy tries to block the blessings that come from giving is through church hurt. Some people get angry or hurt by the church, so they stop giving. They don't like the message the pastor preaches, so they stop giving. Then there are others who backslide and stop giving.

Some stop giving because of discouragement with

their finances. They feel like God isn't answering their prayers for financial breakthrough. They have been declaring, "Money cometh," but nothing is changing. They question where the blessing of God is in their lives. They wonder why they always have a difficult time financially or why it's hard to find good employment. When they do get some kind of overflow, something happens and all the overflow goes into repairing or recovering from an emergency situation—the car breaks down, the roof caves in, or an unexpected illness occurs.

Giving gets even more difficult when they give to someone who is ungrateful or turns around and treats them badly.

These kinds of situations are discouraging and cause some people to want to stop giving. Still, consistent and stable believers do not allow changes in life or the way people act and respond to shake them from doing what has already been set in their hearts. They do what God tells them to do and give how He tells them to give, because they are not looking for man to bless them. They are looking to God to bless them.

We do not give to get the praise and approval of people. We don't give because they treat us nicely. We give because we are being obedient to God. We do not give so someone will treat us right, or so they will like us more. They may never say thank you, but what you did to bless them is between you and God—just like how or if they show gratitude is between them and God.

You do not give in order to place someone in your debt. You are not here to control people. When you give to someone, release the gift. Let the person go on, and leave it between them and God how they live on from there—either filled with gratitude or not. This also means that you should be cautious about whom you accept things from. Some people hold gifts over other people's heads and always bring them up. They want to own others.

Regardless of how other people treat us, their actions should not determine our consistency in giving the way the Lord wants us to. Our hearts should be fixed. A person with a fixed heart is a giver. These individuals will always be givers—cheerful givers. And no circumstance will change that. They know that when they give, it will be given unto them, good measure, pressed down, and running over shall be poured into his bosom. (See Luke 6:38.)

It is more blessed to give than to receive! You must fix your heart in this area, just as you have to fix it in your heart that you will not be a fornicator. That is not a spur-of-the-moment decision you make when faced with a temptation. This is something you have already established. Let's look deeper into how different types of giving and generosity bring the blessings of Psalm 112 into your life.

CHEERFUL GIVING

The Psalm 112 man's giving and generosity shows up twice: in verse 5—"A good man shows generous favor and lends" and in verse 9, quoted at the beginning of this chapter. The word *lends* in the first instance does not necessarily mean that he loans money with the expectation of being paid back, but it also means "gives," as in support, afford, or furnish.[1] Then verse 9 supports this view, saying, "He has given away freely; he has given to the poor."

His giving is directly connected to his graciousness, compassion, and mercy. As we discovered before, this also means he is loving, kind, and gentle—all fruit of the Spirit. His generosity toward and mercy on those who need help is tied to his righteousness, which appears for the third time in this verse as well. And because of his giving, he will have influence and honor.

The Psalm 112 man gives freely and generously. This means he gives without reservation, compulsion, or guilt. He gives without expecting anything in return. *Freely* also means easily, liberally, willingly, and painlessly. The Psalm 112 man could be called a cheerful giver. God loves a joyful, hilarious giver—someone who enjoys giving. Not only should we give, but we should enjoy it while we're doing it. Giving should be something you like to do. You should get pleasure out of doing it. Just as God gets pleasure from the prosperity of His servants, we should get great joy when we contribute to someone's blessing and breakthrough.

GIVING IN THE NATURAL TO BLESS THOSE WHO GIVE IN THE SPIRIT

In 2 Corinthians 9:6–10, Paul uses Psalm 112:9 to encourage the church in Corinth to give to the poor saints at Jerusalem:

> But this I say: He who sows sparingly will also reap sparingly, and he who sows bountifully will also reap bountifully. Let every man give according to the purposes in his heart, not grudgingly or out of necessity, for God loves a cheerful giver. God is able to make all grace abound toward you, so that you, always having enough of everything, may abound to every good work. As it is written [in Ps. 112:9]:

"He has dispersed abroad, He has given to the poor; His righteousness remains forever."
Now He who supplies seed to the sower and supplies bread for your food will also multiply your seed sown and increase the fruits of your righteousness.

Paul uses the example of the Psalm 112 man to tell the church that it can and should be like him who disburses, gives abroad, and gives to the poor. However, the context of this passage goes deeper. The saints in Jerusalem were going through a famine. They were suffering. The Corinthians were sending a love offering to relieve them from the effects of the famine. This giving was prophetic in nature because what was really being taught was the fact that if the Gentiles had received the spiritual blessing and heritage of Israel, then the Jews were to receive the Gentiles' finances—their natural blessings. Since they had received something spiritual from them, the Jewish believers in Jerusalem deserved their natural blessings. This is a principle Paul pointed out to the Corinthians in his first letter: "If we have sown for you spiritual things, is it a great thing if we shall reap your material things?" (1 Cor. 9:11). So basically, whomever you receive from spiritually, you should sow into naturally.

This is the whole principle of supporting ministers and the fivefold ministries—those who bring deliverance, healing, revelation, restoration, and blessing to your life. There are some who miss out on the opportunity to give because of some of the reasons I listed above. They hold out and say, "I don't want to give them anything. Let God take care of them."

Righteous men and women conduct all of their affairs with discretion. (See Psalm 112:5.) They are fixed and established. They are uncompromisingly righteous. I repeat this here because there are ministers who are like wolves in sheep's clothes. They manipulate and steal from people. But the righteous operate with wisdom and justice in all their dealings. They do not make their decisions based on fear of being taken advantage of. They trust God. They are also wise to understand the reward that comes from honoring the man or woman of God.

Of course God will take care of the man or woman of God. Someone will see their fruit and will want to sow into fertile ground. But Psalm 112 believers have already fixed their hearts and minds on when they will give, how much they will give, and to whom they will give. They have discernment. They walk in love and peace and freely give without fear and suspicion. They will not miss out on the blessing and increase that comes from giving this way.

Back to the Corinthian Gentiles. They purposed it in their hearts and gave to the poor Jews from whom they received blessings because Jesus was a Jew and He came through Israel—and He was the Savior of the world. The Gentiles recognized that they were being saved because of this natural nation who kept the Law and the prophets and who brought forth the Messiah. They gave cheerfully and with gratefulness.

Giving natural gifts for spiritual blessing is not a one-time thing. Make room for this in your practice of giving. The Psalm 112 man doesn't get touched one time and, aye, he gives, then after that, nothing. He gives consistently because it is a part of his nature.

You can only do what is inside of you. If it's not in you, it's not coming out. You can say you love people, good ministry, and good worship, but if giving is not part of your makeup, it will not flow out of you. You will be blessed according to the measure you give out. This is why deliverance and good teaching on giving are important. They will help you deal with past ministry hurt, and they will help you apply consistency to your giving. Deliverance will restore the joy you once felt when you gave without reservation.

If there is righteousness in you, you don't have to

force any kind of giving; it will just flow out of you. It's a part of you. It's your nature. You are a new creature.

If you've ever had thoughts like, "Why do I like to give? Why do I like to bless people? Is there something wrong with me?" understand there is nothing wrong with you. You're just a righteous, gracious, compassionate person. You know your God, and you know that He is the One who is pleased when you give. You give because He gave to you.

GIVING AS AN ACT OF WORSHIP

It is really not hard to give when you know who your Father is. God is generous: "Every good gift and every perfect gift is from above and comes down from the Father of lights, with whom is no change or shadow of turning" (James 1:17). When you are saved and a member of the kingdom of God, your heart should be overwhelmed with generosity and gratitude for all God has done. As a Psalm 112 believer, you have a secured place in the kingdom of God where you now experience praise, worship, the Holy Spirit, prophecy, miracles, healings, the presence of God, righteousness, salvation, joy, and rejoicing. Once we get a revelation of who God is and what He has done for us through promises like the one of Psalm 112, our giving becomes an act of worship. Our generosity will flow out of a full heart.

Psalm 96:8 commands us to bring an offering. Worshippers are givers. Worshipping churches are giving churches. Those who experience the glory of the kingdom will give. Churches filled with God's presence will respond with extravagant giving. Giving is not a problem for a worshipping church. Those who respond to God's greatness in worship will have hearts that respond in giving. It is an aspect of worship.

When the wise men came from the East because they saw the star in the heavens, they found the young child Jesus in that place (Matt. 2:9–11). The Bible says that these three kings knelt down and presented Him gold, frankincense, and myrrh. I know you may be very familiar with this story. But it is not just some story we read during the Christmas season. It's a principle: When you come to worship God, you bring Him an offering. You give because you are a worshipper. You give because you honor, respect, and bow to the One you are worshipping. And He is worthy of every gift and every praise you have to give.

179

GIVING AS A COST OF WORSHIP

The king said to Araunah, "No, for I will certainly purchase from you for a fair price. I will not offer up to the Lord burnt offerings that cost me nothing."

So David purchased the threshing floor and the oxen for fifty shekels of silver. David built an altar to the Lord there and offered burnt offerings and peace offerings. Then the land pleaded with the Lord, and the plague was averted from Israel.

—2 Samuel 24:24–26

David, a worshipper, knew the importance of offering. He would not offer the Lord something that did not cost him anything. He understood that giving an offering is about worship. In this passage David had just decided on the land where he would build an altar and the temple of the Lord. He thought about the weight of what he was planning: the site he was standing on was going to be the place of worship for God's people. He thought about all the people who would come from all over the world to this place called the temple of God. So when the landowner offered the land to King David for free, David immediately said, "No, I'm going to buy the property from you, because I will not offer

God something that costs me nothing." Because he respected David, the man wanted to give something as well, and said, "You're the King. I'll give it to you."

David insisted on paying for it because he understood that worship has to cost you something. It has to be a sacrifice. When you come before the presence of God, your worship, your offering must cost you something. Otherwise, it is not a sacrifice.

When you give God something that costs you something, He will give you everything heaven has to offer. As a matter of fact, He gave His only begotten Son. It cost Him everything. Think of what Jesus Christ is worth. God didn't just send a lamb or a bull and offer it.

> For God so loved the world that He gave His
> only begotten Son.
> —JOHN 3:16

It cost heaven its Son, Jesus—Jesus, the Son of God. God gave you something that cost Him something because He loves you.

When we love God, we give Him something that costs us something. I had to check and see if my giving really cost me something. I can give. I'm blessed. I can give a nice offering. But at times, God challenges me: "I want you to give an offering that's going to cost you something." All Psalm 112 believers should hear this challenge every now and then to make sure they are giving in the way that pleases God.

The cost of worship can be different for different people. It might be a dollar, if all you have is $1.50. But if you have a million dollars, one hundred dollars is nothing.

The questions to ask yourself are: Does it cost you anything? Are you really a worshipper? Do you have the heart of a worshipper? Do you really love God? Do you understand the world that has been established by Jesus and the kingdom that you live in? Are you really thankful for the salvation, glory, prophecy, presence, anointing, majesty, and revelation? Are you really thankful for being born again and having new birth?

With all that God has given, no wonder some of us worship so hard. The more revelation you have about who God is, the more you worship. The more you recognize what God has done for you, the more you get into His Word. The more you understand the depths of God's love and His power, the more you touch the anointing of the Holy Spirit. And the more you know about healing, deliverance, prosperity, and the favor and blessing of God, the more deeply you will respond in worship and the more you will give as an act of worship.

Some people are shallow in worship and in their giving because they don't know God. They know about God. But they've never pressed in and learned His depths. They have never encountered the glory of God. They've heard about God. They've talked about God. But they don't really know God. When you really know God, nobody has to make you give to the poor or to the man or woman of God. Your heart will be overflowing with gratitude and thanksgiving. Nobody will have to make you raise your hands. When you really know God, nobody has to make you bow down. You know Him. You know His majesty and His power, His glory and His presence.

Show me a person who doesn't worship, who doesn't give liberally, and I'll show you a person who doesn't know God. They can talk about God. They can sing about God. They can be in a choir. They can go to church. But if they don't worship God, I know they don't really know Him.

AN EXTRAVAGANT GIVER

> ...giving thanks to the Father, who has enabled us to be partakers in the inheritance of the saints in light. He has delivered us from the power of darkness and has transferred us into the kingdom of His dear Son.
> —COLOSSIANS 1:12–13

When Isaiah encountered God, he saw God's train fill the temple. He said, "Woe is me! For I am undone because I am a man of unclean lips, and I dwell in the midst of a people of unclean lips. For my eyes have seen the King, the LORD of Hosts" (Isa. 6:5).

When you encounter God—and I'm not talking about this religious stuff; I'm talking about when you have a God encounter—He changes your life. Nobody can tell you enough about God to cause you to give Him costly worship or be a blessing to the people He brings to you. To be at the Psalm 112 man's level of giving and receiving, you must know God for yourself. When you have experienced God in His glory, you will have to bow down and kneel before the Lord your Maker and honor Him in the way that pleases Him.

DECLARATIONS OF THE BLESSINGS OF GIVING AND GENEROSITY

Thank You, Lord, for Your blessings that come as a result of my giving. I accept Your challenge to give to You and to Your people gifts that cost me something.

I worship You with my giving.

I will be an extravagant giver.

I give to the poor; therefore I am blessed.

Because I give to the poor, the Lord will deliver me in the day of trouble.

Because I give to the poor, the Lord will protect me and keep me alive.

Because I give to the poor, I am called blessed in the land.

Because I give to the poor, when I am sick, the Lord will restore me to full health.

I give freely; therefore I grow richer every day.

I am enriched because I bring blessing.

I give, and it will be given to me. Good measure, pressed down, shaken together, running over, will be put into my lap.

Let my abundance provide for their need.

I sow bountifully; therefore I will also reap bountifully.

Conclusion

COMMIT TO LIVE A PSALM 112 LIFE

T HE BODY OF Christ needs more steadfast and committed believers, those who will not waver, those whose faithfulness testifies and manifests the faithfulness of God. We have too many people who are in one day and out the next. We need examples of consistent lives of faith. You can be the example we need.

There is a blessing to becoming single-minded. To be single-minded is to have one overriding purpose or goal; to be steadfast and resolute; having but one aim or purpose; dedicated, "firm in purpose or belief; characterized by firmness and determination."[1] *Single* in the Greek language is *haplous*, which means "simple...whole; good fulfilling its office; sound, of the eye" (used in Matthew 6:22).[2] A single-minded personality is a whole or sound personality. It is whole and not divided. It is exclusively devoted to God and His Word. A single-minded person has a single heart. He or she is wholehearted, committed, steadfast, and loyal.

These are the characteristics or the trademarks of a stable believer.

> And continuing daily with one mind in the temple, and breaking bread from house to house, they ate their food with gladness and simplicity of heart.
> —ACTS 2:46

> Servants, obey those who are your masters according to the flesh, with fear and trembling, in sincerity of your heart, as to Christ.
> —EPHESIANS 6:5

> Servants, obey your masters in all things according to the flesh, serving not only when they are watching, as the servants of men, but in singleness of heart, fearing God.
> —COLOSSIANS 3:22

The opposite of this is double-mindedness, which often results in backsliding. In other words, having a single mind is key to a person's relationship with God.

The Bible says, "Mark the perfect man, and behold the upright" (Ps. 37:37, KJV). This verse is saying, "Identify the perfect man, the mature man, the whole man." God tells us to mark him, put your finger on him. For the end of that man is peace (shalom)—prosperity, health, wealth, and favor. This is the result of a perfect man. When I say perfect, I don't mean a man who has never made a mistake. I mean a man who is whole and mature—a person who is stable, steadfast, and consistent.

If you can find five people in your life who are whole, consistent, and stable, that will be a miracle. Can you find five people who you can say are complete, mature, consistent, righteous, godly, unchanging, not up and down or in and out, dependable, holy, consistently lovers of God, kind, and gracious? You will find a great number if you can find five.

Many people want the blessing of Psalm 112. They want wealth and riches. They want prosperity. But they don't want to do what it takes to have their hearts purified so they can first prosper on the inside. This should be the goal of every one of us. It's my goal. My prayer is, "Lord, do I line up with the Psalm 112 man?" I cannot say that I've arrived, but I am closer than I was a few years ago. I'm growing. Being consistent and stable is my goal—to be consistent, gracious, kind, and loving; to have a heart that is not corrupted by demons; to have a heart that is not angry, bitter, lustful, or jealous, a heart not full of rejection and hurt, selfishness, self-will, pride, accusation, and fear. Lord, I don't want any of that in me.

God wants consistent, stable people. Recognize that this is not something you do in your own strength. It comes by the grace of God and through deliverance. God stabilizes you. He fills you with the Holy Spirit. But when He does show you any inconsistency in your life, you need to deal with it. Don't ignore it.

Refuse to be a double-minded person. Do not allow double-mindedness in your life. You have access to God's power, grace, and deliverance. Exercise your faith. You can obtain the blessed life of Psalm 112. No matter what life throws at you, you can overcome it all and become a stable, unshakeable, and established believer through Christ.

PSALM 112 DECLARATIONS

Father, I bless You. I thank You for prosperity. I believe in prosperity in my soul and in my life.

Lord, I ask You to lead me to prosper from the inside so that I will be prosperous on the outside. Thank You for making me whole.

Lord, I desire to have a heart that is fixed, established, stable, and steadfast.

I repent of any double-mindedness, instability, foolishness, and confusion I've allowed in my life. I repent for blaming You for the destructive things I allowed into my life through foolish choices and relationships.

Lord, I pray that You would heal me, deliver me, restore me, and make me whole.

I fall out of agreement with all double-mindedness. I loose myself from all rejection, all rebellion, all bitterness, and every spirit that is connected to double-mindedness. I loose myself from lust, fear, depression, discouragement, inferiority, pride, stubbornness, control, and paranoia. I command them to leave my life, in the name of Jesus.

I loose myself from every false personality, every double-minded spirit, in the name of Jesus. I will not be this way.

Thank You, Lord, for delivering me and setting me free. I receive healing, restoration, and wholeness in my body, soul, and spirit.

Thank You, Lord, for uniting my heart. I will not have a divided heart. I will have a united heart to fear You all the days of my life. Thank You, Lord.

———————————

Let the blessings of Psalm 112 be on my life. Let wealth and riches dwell in my house. Let my generations be blessed. Let my righteousness stand out. Let it be remembered forever. Thank You, Lord. I receive it and believe it, in Jesus's name.

Now let's pray together:

> *Heavenly Father, thank You for stability in my life. I will be a stable person. I will not be an unstable person. My heart is fixed and established. I will not have a double mind. I will not walk in double-mindedness and instability. I will not waver. I will be consistent in my giving and living.*
>
> *Thank You, Lord, for giving me the grace and the power to be a godly, consistent, and righteous person. Lord, today I ask You to establish in my life anything that needs to be established. Fix anything in my life that needs to be fixed.*

Thank You, Lord, for Your grace on my life. I receive wealth, prosperity, and blessing in my finances. Lord, thank You for Psalm 112. I receive it. I believe it. Let it be released in my life, in the name of Jesus.

Lord, I commit to living the Psalm 112 life that it may go well with me, that I will be happy and enjoy a long and prosperous life. Amen.

MY PROPHETIC PRAYER AND DECREES FOR YOU

I pray that you will experience a new level of prosperity and wealth.

I pray for the spirit of wisdom to come upon your life.

I decree new wisdom, new grace, new finances, and new prosperity.

I pray that you will be happy when you find wisdom.

I pray that you will increase in wisdom, knowledge, and understanding.

I pray for an impartation of wisdom, knowledge, and understanding to come upon your life.

I pray that God will turn your life around and that wealth, riches, and honor will come into your life.

I pray that God will fill your treasuries, that you will love wisdom, and that you will call wisdom your kinswoman and your helper.

I pray that wisdom will assist you, bless you, and turn your life around.

Let wisdom break poverty, lack, and financial bondage off your life.

Let wisdom cause you to make the right decisions, get involved with the right people, go in the right direction, and live on the right path.

Let wisdom cause you to study to seek out knowledge and understanding.

I pray that wisdom will cause you to forsake sin, anger, wrath, and iniquity, and that you begin to fear the Lord, walk in holiness and righteousness, and follow the right path all of the days of your life.

I pray that wisdom will give you discernment and right judgment so that you can see things clearly and have the prudence to make cautious decisions.

I pray that you will not make rash, foolish decisions but that you will count the cost and be able to weigh things out.

I pray that wisdom will give you the ability to plan, strategize, and look into the future to see what is coming. I pray that wisdom will enable you to walk in the right season.

> *Father, I bless the readers of this book. Do something new and fresh in their lives. Let the anointing of the spirit of wisdom be strong on them as they lead, pastor or minister, conduct business, and commit themselves to their families as husbands, wives, parents, and young people. Father, I pray that their righteousness will live on forever. Increase them more and more, them and their children. May the full blessing and promise of Psalm 112 overtake them, in Jesus's name. Amen.*

NOTES

INTRODUCTION
GOD'S PROMISE TO THE STABLE BELIEVER

1. Blue Letter Bible, s.v. "*tam*," accessed November 12, 2017, https://www.blueletterbible.org/lang/lexicon/lexicon.cfm?Strongs=H8535&t=KJV.

CHAPTER 1
THE CONSEQUENCES OF AN UNSTABLE LIFE

1. Bible Hub, s.v. "*dipsuchos*," accessed November 30, 2017, http://biblehub.com/greek/1374.htm.

2. Bruce E. Levine, "How Teenage Rebellion Has Become a Mental Illness," AlterNet, January 27, 2008, https://www.alternet.org/story/75081/how_teenage_rebellion_has_become_a_mental_illness.

3. Chris N. Simpson, "Freedom From the Deep Hurts of Rejection," NewWineMedia.com, accessed November 30, 2017, http://www.newwinemedia.com/pastorchris/print/Chris_Simpson-Freedom_From_Deep_Hurts_Of_Rejection.pdf.

CHAPTER 2
BLESSED

1. Blue Letter Bible, s.v. *"esher,"* accessed November 26, 2017, https://www.blueletterbible.org/lang/lexicon/lexicon.cfm?Strongs=H835&t=KJV.

2. "The Declaration of Independence," USHistory.org, accessed November 26, 2017, http://www.ushistory.org/declaration/document/.

3. Blue Letter Bible, s.v. *"Běrakah,"* accessed November 27, 2017, https://www.blueletterbible.org/lang/lexicon/lexicon.cfm?Strongs=H1293&t=KJV.

4. Blue Letter Bible, s.v. *"sakal,"* accessed November 27, 2017, https://www.blueletterbible.org/lang/lexicon/lexicon.cfm?Strongs=H7919&t=KJV.

5. Blue Letter Bible, s.v. *"tsalach,"* accessed November 27, 2017, https://www.blueletterbible.org/lang/lexicon/lexicon.cfm?Strongs=H6743&t=KJV.

6. Blue Letter Bible, s.v. *"chayil,"* accessed November 27, 2017, https://www.blueletterbible.org/lang/lexicon/lexicon.cfm?Strongs=H2428&t=KJV.

7. Blue Letter Bible, s.v. *"shalah,"* accessed November 27, 2017, https://www.blueletterbible.org/lang/lexicon/lexicon.cfm?Strongs=H7951&t=KJV.

8. Blue Letter Bible, s.v. *"shalowm,"* accessed November 27, 2017, https://www.blueletterbible.org/lang/lexicon/lexicon.cfm?Strongs=H7965&t=KJV.

9. Blue Letter Bible, s.v. *"ravah,"* accessed November 27, 2017, https://www.blueletterbible.org/lang/lexicon/lexicon.cfm?Strongs=H7301&t=KJV.

10. Blue Letter Bible, s.v. "*koach*," accessed November 27, 2017, https://www.blueletterbible.org/lang/lexicon/lexicon.cfm?Strongs=H3581&t=KJV.

11. Blue Letter Bible, s.v. "*kabad*," accessed November 27, 2017, https://www.blueletterbible.org/lang/lexicon/lexicon.cfm?strongs=H3513&t=KJV.

12. Blue Letter Bible, s.v. "*hown*," accessed November 27, 2017, https://www.blueletterbible.org/lang/lexicon/lexicon.cfm?Strongs=H1952&t=KJV.

13. Blue Letter Bible, s.v. "*ratsown*," accessed November 27, 2017, https://www.blueletterbible.org/lang/lexicon/lexicon.cfm?Strongs=H7522&t=KJV; *The American Heritage Dictionary*, s.v. "favor," accessed November 27, 2017, https://ahdictionary.com/word/search.html?q=favors.

14. Blue Letter Bible, s.v. "*gamal*," accessed November 27, 2017, https://www.blueletterbible.org/lang/lexicon/lexicon.cfm?Strongs=H1580&t=KJV; Dictionary.com, s.v "bountiful," accessed November 27, 2017, http://www.dictionary.com/browse/bountiful.

15. Blue Letter Bible, s.v. "*esher*."

16. Blue Letter Bible, s.v. "*ashar*," accessed November 27, 2017, https://www.blueletterbible.org/lang/lexicon/lexicon.cfm?strongs=H833&t=KJV.

17. Blue Letter Bible, s.v. "*tuwshiyah*," accessed November 27, 2017, https://www.blueletterbible.org/lang/lexicon/lexicon.cfm?Strongs=H8454&t=KJV.

18. Blue Letter Bible, s.v. "*shalal*," accessed November 27, 2017, https://www.blueletterbible.org/lang/lexicon/lexicon.cfm?Strongs=H7998&t=KJV.

19. Blue Letter Bible, s.v. "*eulogeō*," accessed November 27, 2017, https://www.blueletterbible.org/lang/lexicon/lexicon.cfm?Strongs=G2127&t=KJV.

20. Blue Letter Bible, s.v. *"therizō,"* accessed November 27, 2017, https://www.blueletterbible.org/lang/lexicon/lexicon.cfm?strongs=G2325&t=KJV.

21. Blue Letter Bible, s.v. *"euodoō,"* accessed November 27, 2017, https://www.blueletterbible.org/lang/lexicon/lexicon.cfm?Strongs=G2137&t=KJV.

22. Blue Letter Bible, s.v. *"apekdyomai,"* accessed November 27, 2017, https://www.blueletterbible.org/lang/lexicon/lexicon.cfm?Strongs=G554&t=KJV.

23. Blue Letter Bible, s.v. *"empiplēmi,"* accessed November 27, 2017, https://www.blueletterbible.org/lang/lexicon/lexicon.cfm?Strongs=G1705&t=KJV.

24. Blue Letter Bible, s.v. *"diathēkē,"* accessed November 27, 2017, https://www.blueletterbible.org/lang/lexicon/lexicon.cfm?Strongs=G1242&t=KJV.

25. Blue Letter Bible, s.v. *"plēthynō,"* accessed November 27, 2017, https://www.blueletterbible.org/lang/lexicon/lexicon.cfm?Strongs=G4129&t=KJV.

26. Blue Letter Bible, s.v. *"perisseuma,"* accessed November 27, 2017, https://www.blueletterbible.org/lang/lexicon/lexicon.cfm?Strongs=G4051&t=KJV.

27. Blue Letter Bible, s.v. *"autarkeia,"* accessed November 27, 2017, https://www.blueletterbible.org/lang/lexicon/lexicon.cfm?Strongs=G841&t=KJV.

28. Blue Letter Bible, s.v. *"dynamis,"* accessed November 27, 2017, https://www.blueletterbible.org/lang/lexicon/lexicon.cfm?Strongs=G1411&t=KJV.

29. Blue Letter Bible, s.v. *"gibbowr,"* accessed November 15, 2017, https://www.blueletterbible.org/lang/lexicon/lexicon.cfm?Strongs=H1368&t=KJV.

CHAPTER 3
GENERATIONAL BLESSING AND INCREASE

1. Blue Letter Bible, s.v. *"gibbowr,"* accessed November 15, 2017, https://www.blueletterbible.org/lang/lexicon/lexicon.cfm?Strongs=H1368&t=KJV.

CHAPTER 4
MORE THAN ENOUGH

1. Blue Letter Bible, s.v. *"hown,"* accessed November 16, 2017, https://www.blueletterbible.org/lang/lexicon/lexicon.cfm?Strongs=H1952&t=KJV.

2. William Evans, s.v. "wealth, wealthy," *International Standard Bible Encyclopaedia*, accessed November 16, 2017, https://www.blueletterbible.org/search/Dictionary/viewTopic.cfm?topic=IT0009156.

3. Blue Letter Bible, s.v. *"`ashar,"* accessed November 16, 2017, https://www.blueletterbible.org/lang/lexicon/lexicon.cfm?Strongs=H6238.

4. Evans, s.v. "wealth, wealthy."

5. Evans, s.v. "wealth, wealthy."

CHAPTER 5
GRACIOUS AND COMPASSIONATE

1. *Merriam-Webster*, s.v. "grace," accessed November 19, 2017, https://www.merriam-webster.com/dictionary/grace.

2. Blue Letter Bible, s.v. *"rachuwm,"* accessed November 19, 2017, https://www.blueletterbible.org/lang/lexicon/lexicon.cfm?Strongs=H7349&t=KJV.

3. *Merriam-Webster*, s.v. "compassion," accessed November 19, 2017, https://www.merriam-webster.com/dictionary/compassion.

4. *Merriam-Webster* (thesaurus), s.v. "compassion," accessed November 19, 2017, https://www.merriam-webster.com/thesaurus/compassion.

5. Blue Letter Bible, s.v. "*rachuwm*."

6. Blue Letter Bible, s.v. "*tsaddiyq*," accessed November 19, 2017, https://www.blueletterbible.org/lang/lexicon/lexicon.cfm?Strongs=H6662&t=KJV.

7. *Merriam-Webster* (thesaurus), s.v. "righteousness," accessed November 19, 2017, https://www.merriam-webster.com/thesaurus/righteousness.

CHAPTER 6
WISE AND JUST

1. Blue Letter Bible, s.v. "*mishpat*," accessed November 20, 2017, https://www.blueletterbible.org/lang/lexicon/lexicon.cfm?Strongs=H4941&t=KJV.

2. *Merriam-Webster*, s.v. "discretion," accessed November 20, 2017, https://www.merriam-webster.com/dictionary/discretion.

3. Blue Letter Bible, s.v. "*koach*."

4. Blue Letter Bible, s.v. "*malak*," accessed November 25, 2017, https://www.blueletterbible.org/lang/lexicon/lexicon.cfm?Strongs=H4427&t=KJV.

5. Blue Letter Bible, s.v. "*sarar*," accessed November 25, 2017, https://www.blueletterbible.org/lang/lexicon/lexicon.cfm?Strongs=H8323&t=KJV.

6. Blue Letter Bible, s.v. *"shachar,"* accessed November 25, 2017, https://www.blueletterbible.org/lang/lexicon/lexicon .cfm?Strongs=H7836&t=KJV.

CHAPTER 7
RIGHTEOUS FOREVER

1. Blue Letter Bible, s.v. *"tsaddiyq."*
2. Blue Letter Bible, s.v. *"tsaddiyq."*
3. Blue Letter Bible, s.v. *"tsaddiyq."*
4. Blue Letter Bible, s.v. *"tsaddiyq."*
5. Blue Letter Bible, s.v. *"tsaddiyq."*
6. Blue Letter Bible, s.v. *"owlam,"* accessed November 25, 2017, https://www.blueletterbible.org/lang/lexicon/lexicon .cfm?Strongs=H5769&t=KJV.

CHAPTER 8
FIXED AND ESTABLISHED

1. Bible Hub, s.v. *"meshubah,"* accessed December 1, 2017, http://biblehub.com/hebrew/4878.htm.
2. Bible Hub, s.v. *"sarar,"* accessed December 1, 2017, http://biblehub.com/hebrew/5637.htm.
3. Bible Hub, s.v. *"shobab,"* accessed December 1, 2017, http://biblehub.com/hebrew/7726.htm; s.v. *"shobeb,"* accessed December 1, 2017, http://biblehub.com/hebrew/7728.htm.
4. Bible Hub, s.v. *"maad,"* accessed December 1, 2017, http://biblehub.com/hebrew/4571.htm.
5. Bible Hub, s.v. *"stereóma,"* accessed December 1, 2017, http://biblehub.com/greek/4733.htm; s.v. *"stereoó,"* accessed December 1, 2017, http://biblehub.com//greek/4732.htm; s.v. *"stérigmos,"* accessed December 1, 2017, http://biblehub.com

/greek/4740.htm; s.v. "*stérizó*," accessed December 1, 2017, http://biblehub.com/greek/4741.htm.

6. Blue Letter Bible, s.v. "*pistis*," accessed December 1, 2017, https://www.blueletterbible.org/lang/lexicon/lexicon.cfm?Strongs=G4102&t=KJV.

7. Gene Cunningham, "Hebrew Words for Faith," Basic Training Bible Ministries, accessed December 1, 2017, http://www.basictraining.org/print.php?nid=205.

8. Cunningham, "Hebrew Words for Faith."

9. Cunningham, "Hebrew Words for Faith."

CHAPTER 9
GENEROUS

1. *Merriam-Webster*, s.v. "lend," accessed November 30, 2017, https://www.merriam-webster.com/dictionary/lend.

CONCLUSION
COMMIT TO LIVE A PSALM 112 LIFE

1. Free Dictionary, s.v. "single-minded," accessed November 30, 2017, http://www.thefreedictionary.com/single-minded.

2. Blue Letter Bible, s.v. "*haplous*," accessed November 20, 2017, https://www.blueletterbible.org/lang/lexicon/lexicon.cfm?Strongs=G573&t=KJV.